NELSON

THE LIFE OF ALEXANDER SCOTT

Meriden Publications

ISBN 0-9543495-0-4

© Meriden Publications 2003
Originally published by Saunders & Otley, Conduit St. 1842.

How to order: Simply phone MERIDEN PUBLICATIONS
on 01746 765298 or write to: Meriden Publications, 6, Victoria
Road, Bridgnorth, Shropshire, WV16 4LA. UK.

Front cover:
The Death of Nelson, by Arthur Devis, showing Alexander
Scott, first left, rubbing the dying Nelson's chest to ease his
pain.

Published by permission of the Greenwich Hospital
Collection, National Maritime Museum, London.

Printed and bound in Great Britain by
Antony Rowe Ltd, Chippenham, Wiltshire

Introduction

Was Nelson's Chaplain, Alexander Scott, a spy? Even spying for Nelson and Britain seemed somewhat dishonourable to his family. Nelson's continuing fame, and Scott's very close friendship with him overcame this, and Scott's daughter Margaret and her husband, published their recollections of his life in 1842.

Their very rare book, long out of print, can provide you the reader with some evidence to decide for yourself about Scott's role in Nelson's service. It is based on his journals, now lost, and is inevitably biased. Yet it gives a fascinating picture of first hand experience of Britain's greatest sailor and can serve as a background to the bicentenary of Trafalgar in 2005.

Britain's war against France and her allies, depended on more than sea-power alone. British naval strategy often consisted in keeping enemy warships blockaded in port, or enticing them out to the high seas to do battle.

Actual engagements were often heavy bombardment by cannon-fire and the use of fire-arms and the sword. Too many encounters occurred by chance. News travelled so slowly that it took nearly three weeks for news of Trafalgar to reach London! Given the vastness of the oceans, and the limited means of knowing the plans of the enemy and the location of their ships, spying was vital.

The bicentenary of the Battle of Trafalgar will inevitably focus on the continuing charisma of Horatio Nelson, and the irony of his death at the moment of his greatest victory. But Nelson as a brilliant strategist and leader was dependent on many un-sung heroes, and he made enormous efforts to recruit people with talents he needed to guarantee his success.

Was Alexander Scott one of them? It is hoped that the re-publication of these "Recollections" may give Scott the recognition he deserves. You the reader are invited to judge whether or not this can be justified.

H.J.P.

G. Adcock Sc.

LORD NELSON.

From a Miniature by Jackson

Vide page lvi

Men are not always themselves and put on their behaviour with their clothes, but if you live with a man on board a ship for years; if you are continually with him in his cabin, your mind will soon find out how to appreciate him. I could forever tell you the qualities of this beloved man, Horatio Nelson.

I have not shed a tear for years before the 21st October, and since whenever alone, I am quite like a child.

(Alexander Scott writing to a friend)

RECOLLECTIONS

OF

THE LIFE

OF THE

REV. A. J. SCOTT, D.D.

LORD NELSON'S CHAPLAIN,

Πολλῶν δ' ἀνθρώπων ἴδεν ἄστεα, καὶ νόον ἔγνω·
Πολλὰ δ' ὅγ' ἐν πόντῳ πάθεν ἄλγεα.

HOM. OD.

LONDON

SAUNDERS AND OTLEY, CONDUIT-STREET

1842.

PREFACE.

THE following sketch of Dr. Scott's life has been compiled by his daughter and son-in-law, as a tribute of their affection and respect for his memory, and is dedicated to those friends who have encouraged their undertaking. Dr. Scott was so little in the habit of talking over his own eventful career, that even his children were by no means acquainted with all the particulars detailed in this little memoir—the assistance therefore, which has been afforded by the reminiscences of Miss Croft; the Right Hon. Sir George H. Rose, M.P. &c.; Vice-Admiral Sir William Parker, K.C.B.; the Rev. George Townsend, Prebendary of Durham; the Rev. B. Winston, Vicar of Farningham; M. L. Este, Esq., and others, has been highly valuable, and is gratefully acknowledged.

If it be asked what the public has to do with the life of a private clergyman; our answer is, that a man who was three times invited by Lord Nelson to situations of intimacy and confidence, and was honoured by the friendship of that truly noble hero, must have had something more than ordinary about him. If no such marks of distinction appear in our delineation of his character, it must arise from our having brought to the work none of the arts of literature, and from our having been busied in more serious avocations all the while it was in hand.

But we trust that we shall not altogether fail in communicating our impression of Dr. Scott's extraordinary talents and worth, and that many who recall him as the friend of either earlier or later years, will be interested by this connected, though brief record of his life.

Ecclesfield Vicarage,
  May 25, 1842.

CONTENTS.

CHAPTER I.

Birth—parentage—his uncle—goes to the West Indies—Sir Ralph Payne—Charter-house—Cambridge—takes orders—becomes chaplain to the Berwick   1

CHAPTER II.

Mediterranean—first introduction to Lord Nelson—his studies—becomes chaplain to the St. George—Sir Hyde Parker—becomes chaplain to the Britannia—letters to his uncle   18

CHAPTER III.

Returns to England with Sir H. Parker—becomes chaplain to the Queen—West Indies—Letters, &c.—is presented to the living of St. John's, in Jamaica—Journal   39

CHAPTER IV.

Returns to England—cruises in the Channel—Royal George—appointed to the London—Battle of Copenhagen—Lord Nelson—draws up armistice—returns to England   60

CHAPTER V.

Goes out to West Indies—Sir John Duckworth—made chaplain to the Leviathan—visits General Le Clerc—is struck by
lightning and wounded—presented to Southminster—returns
to England 80

CHAPTER VI.

Takes possession of Southminster—illness—becomes chaplain
and secretary to Lord Nelson in the Victory—Mediterranean
—duties as secretary, &c. 94

CHAPTER VII.

Missions into Spain, Sardinia—Magnon—Barcelona sale—mission to Algiers, Sicily, Naples—Journal—pursuit of the
French to the West Indies, and return home 128

CHAPTER VIII.

Re-appointed to the Victory as private secretary, interpreter,
and chaplain—Merton—Trafalgar—death of Lord Nelson—
Dr. Scott returns with the corpse—funeral 178

CHAPTER IX.

Is made D.D. by Royal mandate—disappointed about the
stall at Canterbury—letters from Lady Hamilton, Sir Thomas Hardy, &c.—Mr. Rose—Mr. Canning—Colonel Bosville's—Lady Hamilton........................ 201

CHAPTER X.

Marries—resides at Burnham—his children—manner of life—

death of Mrs. Scott—exertions in his parish—is presented
to Catterick—made King's chaplain............... 226

CHAPTER XI.

Resides at Catterick—literary habits—education of his children
—his library—opinions on Roman Catholic securities. . 254

CHAPTER XII.

Disappointed in Catterick—letters—friends—goes to Southminster—daughter's marriage—illness—Ecclesfield—death
—concluding remarks 278

APPENDIX.

Translation of the Sardinian Poem on Time 297

Note on Roman Catholic Securities................. 300

RECOLLECTIONS

OF

THE LIFE

OF THE

REV. A. J. SCOTT, D. D.

CHAPTER I.

Birth—parentage—his uncle—goes to the West Indies—Sir
Ralph Payne—Charter-house—Cambridge—takes orders—
becomes chaplain to the Berwick.

ALEXANDER JOHN SCOTT was born on the 23rd
of July, 1768, and was baptized at St. Mary's,
Rotherhithe, on the 11th of the following
month.

The earliest member of his family* of whom

* It is probable they had good connections, as Dr. Scott had
inherited an antique silver seal, engraved with the border arms
of the Scott clan, which, it is said, had been taken from the
pocket of one of his ancestors, who was found hanged in a

B

we have any distinct account was his grandfather, who commanded a merchant vessel trading between Scotland and Belfast, and who married a lady from the north of Ireland. They had two sons, Alexander and Robert, both of whom were brought up to a sea life. Robert, the younger, father of the subject of this memoir, became a lieutenant in the navy, but being disappointed of further promotion, retired on half pay, and engaged in ship-building and in the Danish and Russian trade. He married a Miss Jane Comyn, a lady closely related to the family of Vaughan of Golden Grove, with whom, it is said, he eloped from a convent in France, where she was receiving her education.

Only a small fortune was settled on her, and that was never paid; but, in course of time,

tree after the battle of Culloden. This seal he once exhibited to Sir Walter Scott's eldest daughter, whom he met at an evening party at Miss Joanna Baillie's, and playfully claimed kindred with her family. She was very anxious that her father should see this relic, but he was not present that evening, and the opportunity never occurred.

after she had given birth to Alexander John, and two girls, her father made over to her, in lieu of dowry, a small estate at Prince Rupert's Bay, in the island of Dominica. Robert Scott went over to the West Indies for the purpose of realizing this property, but soon fell a victim to the deadly climate of the country; and no money being forthcoming from the estate, Mrs. Scott and her three children, who were residing at Gosport, awaiting his return, were left in a state of the greatest distress and embarrassment, from which, indeed, they could scarcely have extricated themselves, had it not been for the assistance afforded them by her husband's brother.

Captain Alexander Scott had, like Robert, entered the navy at an early age, but had been more successful in his career. He was present at the capture of Quebec by General Wolfe, and he was afterwards employed in *protecting* (tempora mutantur!) the slave trade on the coast of Africa, where by a succession of death vacancies he got such rapid promotion, that he was made commander at an early age.*

At the time when Mrs. Robert Scott and her children became dependent on his kindness, he was in command of a sloop on the home station, and after incurring much difficulty in consequence of his brother's debts, he applied to Lord Sandwich to be removed to the West Indies, where he hoped to settle the family affairs. Unfortunately an opportunity for this did not occur till after a delay of two years, but at that period, namely, in the spring of 1772, he sailed in the Lynx, taking with him his nephew Alexander John, then scarcely four years old. On arriving at Dominica, he found that many debts were due to his deceased brother, but very little could be made of them,

* So remarkable was his rise, that he obtained among the sailors the soubriquet of " God Almighty's Captain "—having twice succeeded to the command of ships from the death of all his superior officers.

and the land at Prince Rupert's Bay was finally sold for £700 to Charles Winston, Esq. the Attorney-General of the island. During the four subsequent years, whilst Captain Scott was employed on the West India station, his nephew was generally living at the house of Sir Ralph Payne,* then governor of the Leeward Islands; and when the American war broke out, and the uncle was promoted to the rank of Post-Captain, and appointed to the Experiment of 50 guns, little "Toby," as Sir Ralph and his lady affectionately called the child, was altogether resigned to their care. They had no children of their own, and he was treated with parental kindness. Lady Payne gave him his first lessons in reading, and to the end of his life she was remembered by him with peculiar affection.

The Experiment, having joined the squadron of Sir Peter Parker, off the coast of America,

---

* Afterwards Lord Lavington.

was engaged on the 28th of June, 1776, in an
attack which was made on Fort Sullivan, in
South Carolina, when Captain Scott lost his
left arm by a cannon ball, and was otherwise
so dangerously wounded, that he was obliged
to retire from active service. After an interval, he was appointed to command the impress
service at Poole in Dorsetshire, where he
married Miss Olive, eldest daughter of John
Olive, Esq., merchant of Oporto, and his
nephew, who had in the meantime returned
to England with Sir Ralph and Lady Payne,
was restored to his guardianship.

The first few years of Dr. Scott's life have
been thus briefly alluded to, partly from our
having but scanty information on the subject,
and also to prevent the confusion that might
otherwise occur betwixt his father and uncle,
as both at one time held the same rank in the
navy. Mrs. Robert Scott had no sooner
become a widow than she was necessarily
separated from her children, as they found

friends to take charge of them, and her son never lived with her again after his return from the West Indies. He was soon sent to school by his uncle, and the following letter is preserved as an amusing specimen of the little scholar's character.

TO CAPTAIN SCOTT.

HONOURED UNCLE,—It is with the greatest pleasure imaginable I sit down to write these few lines to you, therefore I take the liberty of asking you how you do, and I hope you will excuse the faults of a young writer. I dare say you will be anxious to know how long I have learnt to write, which, as far as I can understand, is about eleven months, and for that time I have improved as well as I could, and I suppose I should have written better if it had not been for the Latin, which to me is difficult, and I imagine when you was a little boy like me and learnt Latin, it was the same to you. I

have learnt Latin about eight months, and
now I am in the 8th page of Corderius, and
I hope the next time I have the pleasure of
writing to you, that I shall be in the 30th
page. The next time you see Sir Ralph and
Lady Payne, and likewise Mr. Hick, pray give
my kind love to them all. No more at present
from your ever dutiful nephew,

ALEXANDER JOHN SCOTT.

April 5th, 1777.

In 1778, through Sir Ralph Payne's interest
with Lord Suffolk, young Scott was nominated
by King George III. to a scholarship on the
foundation of the Charter-house. He soon
displayed considerable abilities, but like other
boys occasionally got into disgrace for neglecting his lessons and destroying his clothes; and
Captain Scott, who was at all times rather a
stern disciplinarian, sent a severe reprimand
to him through his mother.

The charge of misbehaviour, however, was not

admitted by her son. He told her he was con-
fident he could learn all the lessons they could
set him; and added, "that *he had never done a
bad thing but once in his life*, and that was when
he ran away from school at Alton."

This was a school to which his uncle had
sent him during the Charter-house holidays,
and the cause of his running away from it was
rather a ludicrous one, but certainly indicative
of the early *gentleman*. The schoolmaster had
wanted to "horse" him in the vulgar old-
fashioned style of flogging, but the proposal
so incensed the little fellow, that he ran home
to his uncle, choosing rather to incur his
anger than submit to the indignity. Indeed,
it would seem that Captain Scott, anxious for
his nephew, who had no dependence in life but
on his own abilities, vexed too by frequent calls
for money from Mrs. Robert Scott and her
mother, Mrs. Comyn, who had taken charge
of her grand-daughters, was hardly just towards
his ward, and occasionally complained of him

at the very time when the masters were prais-
ing his conduct. An interesting proof of his
goodnature is related by his mother in a letter
to Captain Scott. " Toby would have written to
you himself," she writes, " but has met with a
very disagreeable accident at the Charter-house.
He had got a knife in his right hand, and one
of the boys, thinking it was not Toby's, took
it hastily from him, which cut his forefinger
through the nerve. Poor fellow ! the sensation
was so great that he fell down quite senseless,
upon which, the boy who did it, immediately
dragged him to the matrons, and acknowledged
with great distress what he had done. Poor
Toby begged the masters would not be angry
with him, for he was sure his schoolfellow's
heart was so good that he felt more than he
did himself, which I assure you got Toby some
credit."

The vacations he passed generally at his
uncle's, but he was a great deal at Sir Ralph
and Lady Payne's in London ; where, from their

connexion with the Court, he saw the highest society of the day. His intimate friends and com-
panions at the Charter-house were boys of rank
and fortune, who introduced him to their own
family circles; and thus, at an early age, he
was associated with persons in a condition of
life far above his own—a circumstance which
familiarized him with the world, and much
facilitated his intercourse with the great characters among whom he was afterwards thrown.
It was intended that he should go to sea, as
his relations on all sides had done before him;
but he had of late shown very superior talents,
and having obtained from the Charter-house
an exhibition worth £40 a year, it was determined that he should be sent to college. Unfortunately for him, the next necessary consideration was, how this could be done in the
least expensive manner, and his uncle having
made inquiries, the answer of course was, that
the cheapest way of sending him to the university, would be as a sizar. He was conse-

quently entered as a sizar at St. John's College, Cambridge. On his arrival there, his
feelings were deeply wounded by finding himself placed in a position so much beneath that
to which all his former schoolfellows were admitted at St. John's, and other colleges in the
university. He remonstrated with his uncle,
as naturally ignorant of usages and opinions in
our universities, but in vain. Acting as Captain Scott believed he had done, on the very
best information and advice, and, being indis-
posed from professional habits of naval command, to listen to what he deemed the idle
complaints of an insubordinate youngster, he
turned a deaf ear to all his nephew's representations. He reminded him how he had
roughed it in his own career on a more bois-
terous element than the feather beds of college,
and ordered him to " get rid of pride, and do
his duty cheerly." It was more easy, however,
for the uncle to give such advice, than for the
nephew to follow it. No one but an university

man can appreciate the distressing position of young Scott, and enter fully into his feelings. Prudence, no doubt, dictated that with his scanty allowance suited to the situation of a sizar, he should decline associating with his former schoolfellows, who could afford expenses that must infallibly run him into debt. But popular as he was with them, from his lively disposition, talents, and gentlemanlike manners—accustomed always to the best society, and naturally thoughtless about expense, it is no wonder that he should readily meet their advances, and, heedless of consequences, continue in their set.

At that time the studies of Cambridge were almost exclusively mathematical, and St. John's College was peculiarly devoted to that branch of learning. There were no classical "honours" whatever, and but few classical prizes. Hence those who did not distinguish themselves at the mathematical lectures were stamped at once as non-reading men, although they might consume the midnight oil over other studies. A heavy blow, and great discouragement were therefore given to the application and diligence of many young men, who, feeling an insurmountable aversion to mathematics, would yet have read the classics if greater incentives had been offered to that line of study. A change has since happily taken place, and classics, as well as mathematics have now their respective honours. But Scott was one of those who laboured under the disadvantage of former times. The natural bent of his genius was for classical literature and the languages, so that, although at no period of his life idle, he was considered to be so, because he did not adapt himself to the popular study. This, with the fact that he was living beyond his means, made him in bad odour with the tutors, and they set him frequent impositions to write out or get by heart. On one occasion, for returning too late at night from a concert at Huntingdon, he had to learn the three first chapters of St. John in the original Greek, which he accomplished by lying in bed till he could repeat them. It was afterwards seriously debated whether he should not be "rusticated," for, independently of any interest in his own good, no doubt the tutors were mortified at seeing such talents as his, if not actually wasted, employed in studies which gained their college no credit.

The senior dean of St. John's of that day was generally considered a very severe man; and Scott believed him to be much prejudiced against himself—but, to his great surprise, when the other members of the council had given their opinions against him, and sentence of rustication was about to be pronounced, the dean interposed, declaring that the young man had displayed such extraordinary talent in performing the many heavy impositions he had set him, as to prove he was not idle, in the ordinary sense of the word; and he could not be considered insubordinate, as he had never once failed with his task within the prescribed time. This defence averted the punishment, and the opinion expressed by the senior dean (himself a ripe scholar) in favour of Scott's extraordinary talent for languages, was amply borne out by his after career. Indeed, to this worthy man, who had intentionally adapted the impositions which he inflicted to Scott's peculiar faculty, and for the purpose of forcing him to study, Scott felt himself much indebted, and spoke of him in after life with gratitude and respect.

The circumstances of his situation as an undergraduate at St. John's have been dwelt upon, because they had such an important effect on his future destiny. He regretted to the last that he had not been sent to Oxford, where the classics were more read, and he attributed the hardships he subsequently underwent, to his position in college, which disgusted him, and distracted his mind from study ; but these annoyances after all served to bring forward his intellectual powers in a prominent and public manner, by forcing him into a sphere of duty more calculated for their exercise than the situation of a private clergyman could have afforded.

After taking his B.A. degree, he was ordained deacon on the 30th of November, 1791, by Sir William Ashburnham, Bishop of Chichester—his title for orders being a small curacy in Sussex. He remained there more than a year, having been ordained priest the following November. His college debts then pressing heavily upon him—his uncle with some rigour having left him to his own resources on account of them—he accepted the offer of his father's old friend, Sir John Collins, and sailed with him as chaplain to the Berwick of seventy-four guns, in the spring of 1793.

CHAPTER II.

Mediterranean—first introduction to Lord Nelson—his studies—becomes chaplain to the St. George—Sir Hyde Parker
—becomes chaplain to the Britannia—letters to his uncle.

The Berwick was in the first squadron of
the fleet just appointed to the Mediterranean
under the command of Lord Hood. From this
period, Mr. Scott's great facility in acquiring
languages was constantly shown. Although he
had never seriously studied Italian until he
set his foot on board, yet, by the time they
arrived off the coast of Italy, he was sufficiently master of it to be able, on going ashore,
to converse with the natives, to interpret for
the officers of the ship, and to conduct any
negotiations betwixt the commanding admiral
and the Italian maritime states. He also very

soon acquired Spanish. The way in which he set to work when learning new languages (for he did not confine himself to learning one at a time) was such as could only be pursued by a person having a peculiar aptitude and real love for the study. He entirely gave up his mind to them, he kept his journals in them, conversed at every opportunity with foreigners, got pupils out of the ship's company for practice' sake, and read night and day, whenever he could lay his hand on a foreign book. This extraordinary diligence, and an uncommon talent for diplomacy, soon made him a known man in the fleet, and, among other distinguished persons to whom Sir John Collins introduced him, was Captain Horatio Nelson of the Agamemnon. So much struck, even then, was this most illustrious man by Scott's address and abilities, that he conceived at once a strong liking for him, and proposed to him, some time afterwards, on the occasion of Sir John Collins' death, that he should accept the

chaplaincy of the Agamemnon. This kind
offer Mr. Scott respectfully declined, frankly
explaining that, after his services in the Berwick, where he had acted as secretary to Sir
John Collins, as well as chaplain to the ship,
and had been employed diplomatically, he
should not be doing justice to himself in ac-
cepting merely the chaplaincy of a smaller ship.
Captain Nelson quite appreciated this excuse,
but expressed his regret, and added the flattering wish "that some day if he should live to
be an admiral, it might be in his power to
make him an offer more worthy of his acceptance." It is interesting to record this com-
mencement of the acquaintance between Dr.
Scott and our great naval hero, an acquaintance
interrupted for a few years, but destined to be
renewed on a theatre of glory, and to last in
warm and unabated friendship till Nelson
expired in his arms triumphant at Trafalgar.

The Berwick was an unfortunate ship, but
happily Mr. Scott escaped participating in

the disasters which befell her.   He was on
board the Illustrious, when she was dismasted
and reduced to a wreck, in a violent storm in
St. Fiorenzo Bay, in Corsica, in January 1795;
and was on a visit in Leghorn, when she was
captured by the enemy about two months
afterwards. The former event is recorded in
the fragments of one of Scott's journals, kept
in the Italian language, and which among
many other things, contains a catalogue of the
books he was then studying; the commence-
ment of that singularly extensive and varied
library in which during all his subsequent life
he took so much pride and pleasure, and found
so great a solace. The list is most remarkable
from the variety both of languages and subjects
of study which it contains, particularly when
we consider that Scott's age was then not
thirty; that he was a man peculiarly open to
the seductive charms of society, and that this
portion of his life was spent on an element
and with characters most unpropitious to the

pursuits of a scholar. But the truth is, that
whatever were his external occupations, there
was always a life within going on independently of them; scenes, subjects, and persons
were present to his heart and feelings, and
exciting the liveliest interest there, though
utterly apart from the duties of his situation,
which, nevertheless, were zealously fulfilled;
and thus we find during his arduous services
later on in the war, that he was still studying,
still keeping daily memoranda of private feelings; and, (perhaps more striking than all,)
when he was in situations of great personal
danger, either in sickness, or in his secret
services amongst the enemy, or in the more
ordinary risks of a sea life in wartime,—these
are not the chief circumstances recorded in his
diary, but rejoicings over the acquisition of a
new friend, or an old book, or some such individual interest of the simplest and most
characteristic description.

Mr. Scott having been for some time released

from his duties in the Berwick, accepted in
May 1795, the invitation of Admiral Sir Hyde
Parker, to join him as chaplain of the St.
George of 98 guns. To this ship, with the
command of a squadron, Sir Hyde Parker,
had lately been promoted on quitting his station
as captain of the fleet in the Victory, which
was the flag ship of the commander-in-chief.
This was the beginning of a life-long friendship
between Sir Hyde Parker and Mr. Scott, for
the former, as will be seen, became strongly
attached to his chaplain, confiding in him on
all occasions, and always entertaining the most
sincere intentions of regard towards him. Mr.
Scott entered on his new appointment soon
after his return from the visit to Leghorn
before mentioned; a sojourn of many weeks,
which he recalled long afterwards with much
interest and even tenderness. It is probable
that his intercourse with a German clergyman
then residing there, and the present of a German Bible, may have led to his immediately
taking up that language. He commenced a

journal in it at once, without going through
the usual preliminaries of study and reading
—writing it carefully throughout in the text
hand, which as all German scholars are aware
was no easy task. The conciseness unavoidable
in a first effort in a new language must be
excused; indeed, these memoranda do not
properly deserve the name of journals. They
are rather brief notes of the occurrences of the
day, written evidently with very little other
view but the practice they afforded the writer
in expressing himself in whatever new language
he happened to be studying. The opposite
sides of the pages are always filled with extracts
from the books he was reading, and form an
extraordinary accumulation of desultory information. We subjoin a specimen as illustrative
of the monotony of a sea life, and also, to show,
how strong an impression is created in the
mind of

"him that wanders o'er the deep,"

by the charms of a short respite on shore.

1795. May 10. On board the St. George. This day I have begun the German language.

On board and May 11. The wind is not good—we have passed by Corsica—the month of May! it is very beautiful weather.

May 12. On board the St. George. This day very bad weather. What is the heart of man! I think of nothing but my friends in Leghorn.

May 13. The weather is better. I think of nothing but my friends in Leghorn.

May 14. I think of nothing but my friends. The Bête noir always makes me ill.

May 15. I think of nothing, &c. A good wind. We have passed near Sardinia—we see a ship in the distance.

May 16th. I think, &c., The Bête noir, &c.

May 17th. We have passed by Minorca. To-day we have had much fog, we are waiting for the other fleet from England.

May 18. We see a ship coming, which they believe comes from Gibraltar.

c

May 19. We are still waiting for the other ships.

May 20. Four ships have come. They have taken two ships from the French.

May 21. A ship from Leghorn. We continue in the same place, Minorca.

May 22. A ship has gone from hence to Leghorn. I have written four letters.

May 23. Very fine weather, we are still in the same place, and do not know when we shall go away. The Bête noir makes me ill. I think of my friends.

May 24. Beautiful weather—we are still in the same place. It is a pity we cannot avail ourselves of the fine weather in Leghorn. Oh! how happy should I be! Six ships are gone, I believe, to see what the French are doing.

May 25. Always in the same region. I think of my friends.

May 26. In the same place. It is moonlight to-night.

May 27. The weather still good. The sea is calm, but my heart is very restless.

May 28. A ship from Leghorn—but the wind is very strong. To-morrow I hope for some news. What is the world without hope? no more than a lantern without light.

May 29. In the same place—bad weather—and I am unwell.

May 30. In the same place. Weather better. We hear that Lord Hood is not coming, but that the other fleet left England some months ago, and will certainly arrive next week.

May 31, Sunday. I gave the people a sermon. We are still in the same place. I think of my friends in Leghorn.

June 1. We are still in the same place. It is a month ago since my friends dined in the ship. Always unlucky, the consul has broken his shin-bone.

June 2. I have heard no news. To-day, a month ago, my friends dined in the ship. The remembrance of that day gives me great happiness.

June 3. No news. We are still near Minorca.

June 4. This was the king's birthday. We hear nothing new. After supper we made a very great noise with laughing and singing.

June 5. We are every moment expecting the other ships. To day a Swedish vessel passed us. Five ships are come back from Toulon.

June 6. We hear the French fleet is in the port of Toulon. We have been a month at sea. It seems to me a year since I was obliged to leave my friends.

June 7, First Sunday after Trinity. I gave the people a sermon.

June 8. I have been on board another ship, and I have given letters for Leghorn. I think always of my friends. Nothing new will come.

June 9. It is moonlight to-night. Oh, how much I wish to go back to Leghorn!

June 10. There is nothing new. Every day one sees the island of Minorca, and every day

one thinks of one's friends, every day one eats,
every day one drinks—one writes—one reads
—and every evening one goes to bed, where
one dreams of what one thinks of by day.

On the sixth of the month following (July),
we find the fleet in the Bay of Fiorenzo, water-
ing and refitting. Mr. Scott availed himself
as usual of the first opportunity to get on shore,
and went on foot fifteen miles across the country to Bastia, where he was dining with a party
of friends when news reached him that the
fleet was about to weigh anchor. " I must go
back in haste," he says, " for the French have
come to see what we are doing."

In this, however, he was misinformed; the
French had not come to St. Fiorenzo to recon-
noitre the English fleet, which they little suspected of being there, but had been decoyed
forward in chase of a small squadron under
Captain Nelson. " At night we went after the
French," says the journal, and for two or three
days they were in pursuit, but baffled by want
of wind.

July 12. This evening we hear that the
French fleet are near us, but we cannot see
them—we are already prepared to fight.

July 13. We saw the French fleet in the
dawn, about three o'clock; we were ready to
fight, but as the commander-in-chief waited too
long, the wind failed us. The French sailed
near the land, and only seven of our ships
which were foremost, fought. They took a
ship, which began to burn,* we do not know
the reason.

Mr. Scott's uncle had now been promoted to
the rank of rear-admiral, and was residing at
Southampton, where he became an active member of the corporation, and was a warm sup-
porter of the government and principles of Mr.
Pitt. There had been betwixt him and his
nephew. some differences, on account of the
career of the latter at college; but Mr. Scott
had so completely shown that the errors of

---

* This was the Alcide, from an explosion of combustibles in
her foretop. Four hundred of the crew perished in her.

those days arose from no defect of principle;
he had also paid his debts there so honourably,
without the assistance of any one, and was be-
having towards his mother with so much generosity, and all this out of his pay, and the
prize money, which in the chances of war fell
to his share, that Admiral Scott could not with-
hold his forgiveness. It must also have gratified him to find how much attention and confidence Mr. Scott was gaining in the fleet, where
he was employed confidentially by some of the
most distinguished officers, apart from his situation as private secretary to Sir Hyde Parker,
to which he had been appointed; and he had
particularly attracted the notice of Sir Gilbert
Elliot, Viceroy of Corsica, who, besides offering
him the chaplaincy of Bastia, wished him to
live in his family, and become tutor to his sons.
This offer he would have accepted, but for the
extreme regret Sir Hyde Parker showed on the
occasion—begging him with tears in his eyes
not to leave him. Scott therefore declined Sir

Gilbert Elliot's proposal; but often lamented
the opportunity he thus lost of visiting the
eastern world, Sir G. Elliot having been subsequently appointed Governor-general of Bengal.

TO ADMIRAL SCOTT.

H.M.S. Britannia, St. Fiorenzo Bay,
January 22nd, 1796.

MY DEAR UNCLE,—My last to you should have
been dated the 12th inst.; Lord Hervey had
been dead some days when I wrote, intelligence
of which I did not receive till after my letter had
been forwarded on board the flag. The fleet
anchored here on the 14th instant, and found
everything quiet in Corsica; great reports of a
truce between the Austrians and the French
on the Rhine; and, as is pretended, strong
symptoms of a general peace. The viceroy
gave a ball and supper to the fleet and army on
the queen's birthday, which, I understand, was
well attended. We all moved into this ship on
the 16th instant; Captain Foley is still with

us, and likely to continue. Sir John Jervis
has employed me lately in translating his Italian papers, some of which are of the most material consequence. I had the honour of dining
with him on the 20th instant, and was received
very courteously by him. Captain Calder has
been very kind to me; your letter to him he
has not as yet received.

I have just received a letter from a Mr. Thomas, the rector of Woolwich. His uncle, the
late Bishop of Rochester, having no children,
has left him a large fortune, in consequence of
which, he has bought the house of Sir Peter
Dennis at Maize Hill, near Greenwich, and
retired from Woolwich—he promises, however,
to secure the curacy of his living for me at the
end of the war, and appoints £80 per annum as
my salary. The duty is certainly very fatiguing,
as the whole day is from morning to night filled
up in discharging the duties of so extensive a
parish as it is; but, as I got through it very
well when I was last at Woolwich, for the space

of a week, I do not doubt but I could continue
to do so for a longer term; I have, therefore,
thanked him for his offer, and joyfully accepted
it; and I likewise hope to get the nearest guard
ship, which I believe is at Chatham, through
the interest of Sir Hyde Parker and yourself,
if you approve my plan. Sir Hyde is very intimate with Admiral Young, and Captain Campbell is the great friend of the Seymour family,
and I am sure they will both assist me with
more pleasure, now that I am reconciled to my
friends.

Allow me again to make an apology for writing so slovenly. The German papers are just
arrived from Leghorn, and I am about to trans-
late the news for Sir Hyde. They contain
nothing but what is old news to you. Captain
Young is now going home with the viceroy's
despatches, and I have only time to subscribe
myself, ever,   Your obliged nephew,

And attached humble servant,

A. J. Scott.

Sickness compelled the two Neapolitan ships to quit the fleet yesterday evening, and go to Naples. The Agamemnon is sent to bring troops from Trieste to Corsica. The Tancredi is expected from Naples every day to join the fleet. Nothing is settled with regard to the Bastia chaplaincy.

TO ADMIRAL SCOTT.

Britannia, Leghorn Roads,
February 10th, 1796.

MY DEAR UNCLE,—From the 22nd ultimo, when I had last the pleasure of writing to you, the fleet remained at Fiorenzo until the 9th inst., on which day we put to sea, and steered for this port, where we have now been at anchor about twenty minutes. During our stay in Corsica nothing material occurred, except the arrival of a French cartel from Toulon; which bringing us only forty-nine English, was suspected of other views than the exchange of pri-

soners; and, after receiving her quota of French
in return for the number she brought, was ordered to put to sea immediately. Early this
morning, Admiral Waldegrave in the Barfleur,
with the Egmont, Zealous, and Bombay Castle,
parted company, and steered to the westward;
the destination of his squadron is a secret.
Cagliari has planted the tree of liberty, and
massacred several of the nobles; the north
part of the island is also in the same state of
revolt. It appears now that there has always
existed a French party in Sardinia. But I am
happy to add that only Cagliari and the north
part of the kingdom are infected with this republican mania. Captain Calder has as yet
never received the letter you sent him. I am
much indebted to him for the marked attention
which he has been pleased to show me. I
dined again a few days since with Sir John
Jervis; your name was mentioned, and Sir
John regretted, in a *courtier-like* manner, that
you were not employed. I purpose to subjoin

to this letter a copy of my letter to Sir Gilbert
Elliot, in answer to his offer of appointing me
chaplain at Bastia, On this occasion I went
so far as to assure Sir Hyde that I would not
think of leaving him, except by his particular
desire, and that, should he be ordered home in
a frigate, I hoped he would take me with him.
I trust you will approve of my conduct on this
occasion, especially when you hear that it has
connected me still closer with a man to whom
I was under great obligations. I believe the
post goes from Leghorn this evening, I shall
therefore conclude with assuring you that I am
with the most heartfelt sincerity, and truest
respect,

Your obliged nephew,

And grateful humble servant,

A. J. SCOTT.

P. S.—It should be mentioned that I am
wholly unacquainted with the value of the
Bastia chaplaincy.

TO SIR G. ELLIOT, KNIGHT OF THE BATH, &c.

Britannia, February 3, 1796.

SIR,—I have the honour to make my most respectful acknowledgments to your Excellency for
your kind intentions in my favour, which were
made known to me this morning by Sir Hyde
Parker, in answer to which I am to acquaint
your Excellency that I feel myself, as well from
gratitude as from inclination, so much attached
to Sir Hyde Parker, that nothing, however
advantageous, can induce me to quit him. I
beg leave to assure your Excellency that I en-
tertain the highest sense of gratitude for this
flattering proof of your notice of me, and that
I shall ever remain,

With respect, &c. &c.

A. J. SCOTT.

CHAPTER III.

Returns to England with Sir H. Parker—becomes Chaplain
to the Queen—West Indies—Letters, &c.—is presented to
the living of St. John's, in Jamaica—Journal.

THE high place which Mr. Scott now occupied
in Sir Hyde Parker's esteem, is further proved
by his being selected to accompany him to
England, and intrusted with the object of their
journey, which was of the most private and
delicate nature. They travelled overland from
Leghorn to Hamburgh by way of the Tyrol,
with which country Mr. Scott was delighted.
The comparison, he says, betwixt the best of
the Italians and the Tyrolese, is infinitely in
favour of the latter ; and he remarks the superior neatness and comfort in their houses, the
industry of the peasantry, and their thriving

farms, "where the Englishman's eye is glad-
dened with the sight of cattle fat and sleek,
as those in his native land." They crossed
from Hamburgh to Harwich, and it is to be
regretted that only a very imperfect recollec-
tion exists of their journey from thence up to
London, of which Dr. Scott made such an
excellent story. His place being occupied in
Sir Hyde's carriage, he engaged to ride post,
and to keep up with four horses driven at such
speed as a sailor proverbially likes. The
weather was hot, the roads dusty, and Scott
utterly out of practice in riding; but if his
horse turned restive, or he himself flagged from
fatigue, Sir Hyde's voice from the window
rallied him on, until at last he was glad to tie
a handkerchief round his loins for support,
and in this state he arrived at Ingatestone,
where they rested for the night. The Admiral
never dreamed that Scott would join them
again in the morning, but when the carriage
came to the door, he was already in the saddle;

and having refreshed himself with a warm bath
at his hotel in London, he attended the dinner-
party in Cumberland Place the same evening,
and the Opera after.

In a few days he writes the following letter
to his uncle, which, like its predecessors, be-
trays evident symptoms of that constraint, and
almost fear, which Admiral Scott's peculiar
character excited, and of which Mr. Scott, as
being so much indebted to him, was the more
especially susceptible.

TO REAR-ADMIRAL SCOTT.

Ibbotson's Hotel, London,
June 4, 1796.

DEAR SIR,—The apparent negligence of my
letter of yesterday, may probably have occasioned you some uneasiness ; but I thought it
better to write in the hurry of the moment,
rather than not write at all. I dined with
Lady Parker yesterday. Sir Hyde proposes

upon Sir Harry's return from the Isle of Wight
with his children, to go into Suffolk for a few
days. His stay in England will be very short,
as Lord Spencer tells him his presence is
actually necessary in the Mediterranean, and
that he hopes his private affairs will soon permit him to return thither, adding at the same
time, how happy he was in having so able an
officer ready to take the command of the Mediterranean fleet, in case of any accident attend-
ing Sir John Jervis. Sir Hyde is to return
by sea, and means to take me with him, but
he cannot as yet fix the term of his stay in
England.

I should certainly not have been at this end
of the town at an expensive hotel, were I not
with the Admiral. To-day he means to intro-
duce me to Sir A. Hammond, who has particularly desired to see me, but I know not on what
account. On Monday evening, if you do not
forbid me, I shall come down to Southampton
for a few days. I should set off this evening,

but I conclude you would wish me to see Lady
Lavington, if possible; and it is also requisite
that I should see Mr. Thomas, at Maize Hill,
Greenwich, to whom I am under obligations.
Will you forget for a few hours the many
errors I have committed, and receive me as
your nephew,

And grateful humble servant,

A. J. SCOTT.

The destination, however, of the admiral and
his chaplain, was suddenly changed from what
was proposed in the foregoing letter. Owing
to the continued hostilities with France, and
the increased danger to our colonial possessions
in the West Indies, from the presence of the
emissaries of the Convention, it was very
necessary to maintain an efficient naval force
in that quarter; and the command on the
Jamaica station becoming vacant at this moment, it was given to Sir Hyde Parker, who

accordingly went out thither in the autumn
of 1796, hoisting his flag in the Queen as
Commander-in-chief. In this appointment he
was accompanied by Mr. Scott in his usual
capacities.

TO REAR-ADMIRAL SCOTT.

H.M.S. Queen, Fort Royal Bay,
Martinique, Oct. 2, 1796.

MY DEAR UNCLE,—The Beaulieu frigate sails to-
night or to-morrow morning for England, and car-
ries home Admirals Christian and Pole. Since
my last, nothing material has occurred. The
Pelican brig, a few days ago, beat off a French
frigate called the Medea, and Capt. Searle,
who commanded her, has acquired great credit
by it. Victor Hugues goes on in the same
style—sometimes remarkably civil, at other
times as much the reverse. The other day, he
sent for all the surgeons and medical people
whom he has at Guadaloupe as prisoners of

war, and told them that understanding the English troops and squadron were getting healthy, through the great scarcity of men of their profession, he purposed forthwith to send them back to their countrymen. This was only a *jeu d'esprit* to amuse the mobility, for he has never thought of performing it in earnest : indeed he too well knows how sickly we are.

The noyeau is no longer to be had good here; the great demand for it by the English army and navy, having caused it to be adulterated. The house of Grandmaison no longer exists; the Revolution having scattered the family. On these reasons I have forborne to send you any; and as I go so little ashore, I have no chance of procuring any better by cultivating an acquaintance with the people of the Island. I most earnestly wish to hear soon from you; and I most earnestly pray that you, with my aunt and family, are all in good health, and may continue to remain so.

It is impossible to say what we shall do here;
our situation is peculiar. Probably despatches
from England will elucidate matters. The
Rattler sloop is arrived from Spithead; but
the despatches brought by her only tend to
prepare Admiral Hervey for Sir Hyde's arrival.
I wish anxiously to get to sea again: anything
but this disagreeable and unhealthy bay. Had
I been prepared with any letters to your friends
in Dominique, I certainly would have gone in
one of the frigates, and remained there a week
or a fortnight. Two families, emigrés from
Guadaloupe, visit us. The Admiral is well,
and fond of making parties of ladies; though
they for the most part speak bad French, and
seem wholly enervated by the climate. I have
been ashore once or twice to visit them with
Sir Hyde, but I never go ashore without fear.
However I am not the only frightened one—
many bolder are so, and I am sorry to say not
without apparent reason. I beg my duty and
respects to my aunt—my love to my cousins;

and best remembrances to Mrs. Sandford and her boy.

I remain, dearest uncle,

With heartfelt love and gratitude,

Your nephew,

A. J. SCOTT.

TO REAR-ADMIRAL SCOTT.

Queen, cruising off Cape François, in the
Island of St. Domingo, December 6th, 1796.

My DEAR UNCLE,—My last was dated October the 2nd, since when little has occurred which can afford you any entertainment. On the 22nd October, the ship's company being very sickly, we left Fort Royal Bay, and went over to Gros Islet Bay at Saint Lucie. This change of air was found of great service to the people, On the 29th we left Saint Lucie, and returned to Martinique, but anchored in Caz-navire Bay, which is thought to be a healthy situation. On the 31st a cutter arrived from England with despatches, and on the 1st of November we

sailed for St. Domingo with the Valiant, Carna-
tic, and Thunderer in company. On the 6th,
we took a Spanish brig from the Caraccas, bound
to Spain. I say *took*, but it should rather be
detained. The cutter above mentioned brought
orders to detain and *distress*, but not to capture; but we daily expect authority to do the
latter, as we have received intelligence (although it is not fully ascertained) that a
Spanish frigate has arrived at Port Rico with
an account of the declaration of war. On the
12th ult. we anchored in Cape St. Nicholas
Mole, and found there the Dictator, 64. The
rest of the squadron under Admiral Bligh in
the Brunswick, with the Canada, Leviathan,
Hannibal, and Alfred, we had fallen in with on
the 12th, and they accompanied us to the
Mole. The Admiral on the 19th ult. despatched three sail on a cruise, and on the 20th,
the rest of the squadron, consisting of seven
sail of the line, sailed for this cruising ground,
where we are hourly expecting Mr. Richery

from America. Unfortunately the Brunswick lost her main-topmast a few days ago, and part of the maintop being also carried away, she was forced to go into port. I am happy to have in my power to inform you that I have had three attacks of a fever. Twice at Martinique, which were only slight touches, but the latter at Cape St. Nicholas was very severe, as the doctors say. I am now only able to crawl, but I eat so heartily and sleep so soundly that there is no fear of me. After this I shall be perfectly acclimaté. This is the first time that I have attempted to write since my illness, and therefore you must forgive any inattentions or inaccuracies you may meet with. I saw a great deal of Captain Hervey at Martinique, and received many attentions from him. He is on a separate cruise at present. I cannot speak too highly of Sir Hyde's attention and kindness to me during the time I was confined. Indeed, I experience his regard for me at all times, but I was more particularly sensible of it then. I hope my aunt and family are well, and I beg you will be kind enough to present to them my duty and affection. Mrs. Sandford and her little boy, and the worthy Mrs. Cobham, I trust are well, and I beg my respects to them. I shall write again the first oppor-tunity. Since my last none has occurred till the present. Wishing you health above all things,

I am, &c.,

A. J. SCOTT.

To a young man of Mr. Scott's ardent dis-position his employments on this station soon became highly interesting. Whilst on board, he was constantly living with the Admiral, and their frequent capture of Spanish vessels af-forded him a double source of gratification; for, independently of the amusement and fur-ther practice in languages which he derived from the examination of the ships' papers, he had his share also of prize money, which he lavishly expended in the formation of his

foreign library. The value of some of these
prizes was very great. He mentions one captured by the Amphion and Alarm, whose
invoice amounted to nearly £200,000, and
that Admiral Parker and the two Captains
would at least have each £25,000. Such large
sums, of course, suggest no fair notion of the
chaplain's very minute proportion. Their intercourse with the Spanish Main enabled him
to acquire a thorough proficiency in that language, and his journals of this date are daily
interspersed with extracts from both Spanish
prose and poetry. On the Admiral's going to
reside at Cape Nicholas Mole in St. Domingo,
which they found a very sickly station, Mr.
Scott continued living with him as his private
secretary, at the same time doing the duty of
the flag-ship in port. And, from being the
only clergyman on the spot, he was compelled
to attend various executions of the crew of the
Hermione and others which took place there.
On one of these occasions four men were

hanged for piracy. When he was in attend-
ance upon them after they were condemned,
they exhibited so much good feeling, that he
was greatly interested for them. They were,
moreover, all young, and in person the finest
models of seamen that he had ever seen of
any nation. Nothing could be more distressing to Mr Scott than the necessity of being
present at these dreadful scenes. His nature
shrunk at all times with peculiar tenderness
from the sight, as well as the infliction of
suffering, and on the occasions alluded to, there
was everything in the ceremony also to excite
the feelings. He described it as awful. The
firing of the signal gun—the smoke rising to
conceal the death struggles—and, as it cleared
off, the lifeless bodies swinging from the yard-
arms. He never raised his eyes from the deck
till all was over, and was inexpressibly thank-
ful to escape from the scene. In a memorial
of these services he uses the expression, " I
was *compelled* to attend," which may best
llustrate how unwelcome the office had been.

He used to relate an anecdote of himself
about this time, which, in these days of wonder
and mesmerism, may perhaps serve to throw
some additional mystery round the already dark
subject of animal magnetism. Being asleep
one morning in his cot, he dreamed of a boy
who had been at school with him at the Charter-
house, but with whom he had never been on
very friendly terms. The dream was a vivid
one, and he saw the boy distinctly before him,
as he had known him at school, fifteen years
before ; a singular circumstance, as since he
left school, he had neither seen, heard, nor
thought anything about him. On awaking, he
saw standing over him, as if watching his sleep,
a young man, whose features were perfectly
unknown to him. What was his astonishment
when the stranger introduced himself as the
very boy of whom he had been dreaming !

On the evacuation of St. Domingo by the
British forces in 1798, when Sir Hyde Parker
went to Jamaica, and took up his residence at the

Pen—a country house near Greenwich, which
was provided by the local government, and very
pleasantly situated between the latter place and
Kingston—Mr. Scott accompanied his patron,
and lived in his family. The profuse hospitalities
which were dispensed at the Pen soon introduced
Scott to all the principal residents in the island
—many of whom became much attached to
him, and he was constantly involved in all the
gaiety of visiting.   Nevertheless, those who
still remember him at this period, testify that
besides his favourite study of languages, he was
still keeping up his classical knowledge, and
that line of reading appropriate to his clerical
profession.   His own ardent mind, however,
found no satisfaction, either in his opportunities or exertions at this period.   He complained
to his uncle that he could acquire but little
information in such a country, that the climate
disabled him from serious application, and be-
numbed all his mental faculties.   Nevertheless,
he adds, " I look upon my collection of books

as my greatest hope of future comfort. I am
constantly adding to it ; I have here with me
now nearly six hundred and fifty volumes."
He continues, " I must beg leave to repeat my
anxiety about a large box of books sent home
in the Adventure, more than a year ago. I
had them packed in a large black box, and the
direction was painted with white paint, ' Rear
Admiral Scott, Southampton.' As they were
all old books, I cannot think the Custom-house
has seized them." By the interest of Sir Hyde
Parker with the governor of Jamaica, he was
now presented to the living of St. John's in
that island, the value of which was about £500
a year, and it was tenable with his naval chaplaincy. Of his residence at St. John's, which
was healthily situated in the interior, near the
mountains, he always spoke with much pleasure. His improved circumstances admitted
of his enjoying an establishment of his own
there, and among his resources, was the driving
a curricle with a pair of fast horses, of which

in later life, he used to joke with the greatest
goût and delight. In this manner he would
sally from his retirement and books, either to
a sojourn with the Admiral, or on a visit among
his island acquaintance, or to a dinner with his
friends at Port Royal anchorage, where he was
always gladly hailed as an agreeable messmate.
A record in the journal also makes mention of
his playing a great deal on the harpsichord—
and it may be as well to observe here, that
among Mr. Scott's many pursuits, a very favourite one was music. His collection of mu-
sical compositions was begun as early as that of
books; and, during his visits at Leghorn and
Hamburgh, he not only increased his stock by
the valuable addition of Mozart's operas in
score, and the best modern music of the day,
but copied himself in very beautiful manuscript
a selection of waltzes not known in England,
but which, from their great delicacy and beauty,
evidence, beyond a doubt, his taste and feeling in the art.

We give a few extracts from his diary of this time, which was still kept in German.

Jan. 6, 1800. At St. John's. To buy these books, namely, Covambias, Quevedo, Gracian, Empresas Politicas, and the Princes of Esquilache; they are all Spanish books; also Don Antonio de Solis, also Gongora.

Jan. 7. I am still in the country. Petrarch, in a letter to Hugolin de Rossi, Bishop of Parma, says, " there is not a single person whose reputation is wounded by my tongue;" what a charitable thought !

Jan. 8. I am at Olive Mount, where I arrived yesterday evening at 8 o'clock. It is twelve miles from Lloyd's.

Jan. 9, 10. Yesterday evening I left Mr. Pleydell's, and am come to sleep at Mr. Douglas's.

Jan. 11. I am at Mr. Douglas's—the spring overflowed and was called Perilous, now Peerless Pool. N. B. To call at Mr. Grant's, at

Water Mount, to baptize a brown man. John Norman, chosen Lord Mayor in 1454, changed the custom of riding to Westminster, to that of going by water.

Jan. 12. I spent the last night in dancing at Dr. Tulloch's.

Jan. 13. Slept at the doctor's. To-day I came to Mr. Oliver's to baptize his children.

Jan. 14. Came back to Dr. Tulloch's. To buy Baxter's Metaphysics; founded upon the physics of Newton.

Jan. 15. At Mountain river.

Jan. 16. Dined at the barracks, and slept at Mr. Douglas's.

Jan. 17. Dined at Mr. Grant's—baptized some persons.

Feb. 8. Sent away to England some books by Mr. Herbert, namely, Russian Dictionary and Grammar, Arabic Grammar, Euler's Letters, Bemetzrieder on music; and Mr. Thomas will send me a Sclavonian Dictionary

and Grammar, a Turkish ditto, and Kaims's
Sketches of Man. N. B. Sclavonia is the
ancient Illyria. Apes and men degenerate
least out of their native element.

CHAPTER IV.

Returns to England—cruises in the Channel—Royal George—
appointed to the London—Battle of Copenhagen—Lord
Nelson—draws up armistice—returns to England.

In the autumn of this year, Sir Hyde Parker,
being relieved in his command by Lord Hugh
Seymour, returned to England in the Trent
frigate, accompanied by Mr. Scott, who had
leave of absence from his benefice on account
of his health. On their arrival, he parted from
the Admiral, who was in the heat of preparation for his marriage with Miss Onslow, and,
after passing a very delightful month of recre-
ation at Hamburgh, he rejoined him in the
Royal George, where Sir Hyde had just become
second in command of the Channel fleet. Nothing very interesting occurred during this

short cruise, as they happily escaped the snare
prepared for them by the French, who omitted
to light up their lighthouses on St. Mathieu
and Ushant, when the fleet appeared off their
coasts.

Mr. Scott would not have remained long
away from his living, but for another still more
important command with which his patron was
so soon invested—being made chief admiral of
a large fleet destined for the Baltic. It may
be well to remind the reader, that the Emperor
Paul of Russia had completely failed England
in the co-operation she had been led to expect
from him against the encroachments of Napoleon Buonaparte. That crafty usurper had
artfully worked on the vanity of Paul, and
attached him to himself by some plausible concessions, and especially by encouraging him in
viewing as a personal insult the refusal of this
country to cede Malta to Russia, which Paul
had been wild enough to demand. This last
manœuvre made the Emperor ready for any

pretext for a coalition against the British government; which the active diplomatic spirit of
the First Consul soon stirred up. The right,
during war-time, to search neutral vessels at sea,
and other maritime privileges claimed by England, and accorded to her by Russia, and every
naval power in Europe, was directly opposed to
Buonaparte's favourite scheme of the liberty of
the seas, and prevented France from obtaining
unmolested, that supply of naval stores from
the Baltic which was necessary for her fleets.
To urge, therefore, the already irritated Paul
into acts of violence against our ships in the
Russian ports, and through him to persuade or
threaten Denmark and Sweden into regarding
our dominion of the seas as an oppressive interference with their commercial advantages, was
the policy of France, and not very difficult of
accomplishment. Injuries were committed on
our ships, retaliation followed by the seizure of
all vessels belonging to the three northern
nations found in our harbours, and the quick

result of these hostilities was, that at the beginning of the year 1801, England had not only
to dare the enormous military power of France,
but a confederacy by sea, of Russia, Denmark,
and Sweden, with France and Prussia hasten-
ing to assist them. Mr. Addington, the British minister, acted at this crisis with the utmost
energy, whatever opinions may be held as to
the line of policy he pursued. Sir Hyde Parker, as a senior and distinguished officer, was
at once appointed to the chief command of a
fleet of above fifty sail of various descriptions,
with orders to proceed to the Baltic; and he
was only unfortunate in the appointment thus
conferred on him—if misfortune it could be
called by a generous mind—that second to him
was the man who has eclipsed, not merely his
own country and his own age in naval renown,
but has thrown a lustre altogether unparalleled
over the naval history of the world by the glory
of his achievements.

Sir Hyde removed with his captain and offi-

cers into the London. Mr. Scott was made
chaplain to the ship, and interpreter and trans-
lator of languages to the expedition, by a war-
rant from the commander-in-chief; but, unfortunately for him, the latter appointment being
without authority from the admiralty, was considered as the admiral's own private arrangement, and never recognised by the lords com-
missioners. Before Scott left London, in due
preparation for the services he expected would
be demanded of him, he purchased a Danish
Grammar and Dictionary, for he had not yet
studied that language, and he fell to work immediately on taking his place on board. He
also provided the Elemens de la langue Russe,*
published by the Imperial Academy of Sciences

---

* This book contains the following entry, " This book
kindly lent by Dr. Rogers, late of St. Petersburgh, to John
Sewell, 32, Cornhill, for the express purpose of accommodating
the Rev. — Scott, going in the present armament to the
North. Sewell procured it from Dr. R., with intent to have
it translated into English, and printed, in which work Mr.
Scott can probably assist.—32, Cornhill, 4th March, 1801."

at St. Petersburgh. For obtaining a knowledge of the former language, his previous acquaintance with German was, of course, of the
greatest use, and in a few days he commenced
keeping his diary in Danish as well as German.

The London sailed from Portsmouth on the
3rd of March, and, being detained a few days in
the Downs by contrary winds, arrived at Yar-
mouth on the 9th, where the whole fleet ren-
dezvoused. They sailed in company on the
12th, and on the 18th were in sight of the coast
of Norway, at the entrance of the Cattegat.

TO REAR-ADMIRAL SCOTT.

March 18th, 1801, off the Cattegat, London.

MY DEAR UNCLE,—I am not aware that I shall
have it in my power to send you this, but suppose
that the Admiral will naturally despatch something on the eve of our entering the Sound.
The Elephant has just joined us, by which ship
I have received a letter forwarded to me at Yar-
mouth from Southampton. On the inward

margin of my letter I perceive that the Ency-
clopædia has reached you, a matter which
gives mé infinite pleasure. I wrote to you
by the Alecto fire-ship, which was disabled,
and forced to make for Leith, although by a
sudden shift of wind it is most probable she is
gone to the Humber. I this moment learn that
something will go in to-morrrow morning. It
is now late, I must therefore only assure you
of my most respectful and affectionate attachment, and with love to all beg you to believe
me, &c., &c.,

                                A. J. SCOTT.

I feel disappointed at not hearing from
Spring Hill by every possible opportunity.
Surely some one might throw a few minutes
away as a token of remembrance of me. I
have received a very friendly note from Captain
Walker, but have not yet been so fortunate as
to meet him. It only reached me after the
fleet had unmoored. It is impossible for me

to impress upon your mind more strongly than you feel, the importance and risk of our present expedition. God send us with honour and credit through the business! We are all made up of anxiety and determination to do something. Notwithstanding all this, and even the *king's illness*, I am still more uneasy about my own situation and worldly prospects. This is for my aunt, who is so very patriotic, to whom I make my best duty and love over and over again. To Mrs. Sandford, Ben, Eliza, Mary, Caroline, everything that a warm heart can say. Are the books from Portsmouth arrived? I trust the girls (I include Mrs. Sandford and Mrs. Scott) will tell me what they think of my library, at least this last lot. Do recall me to the remembrance of Lady Irvine, Mrs. Walker, and Miss Grovesnor, whom entre nous I prefer to most of my London fal lal acquaintance. I have written thus far by sudden starts, and must now conclude my letter, however incoherently written.

TO REAR-ADMIRAL SCOTT.

Cattegat, five leagues off the Kull Point,
March 21st, 1801.

MY DEAR UNCLE,—The frigate has not brought
us the ultimatum of the Danish Court, which
we hourly expect. Should it be unfavourable
we shall commence hostilities whenever the
wind permits us to pass the Sound. We are
now at anchor—a heavy swell running—the
wind S. W. or thereabouts. The London was
nearly lost yesterday on a shoal with only nineteen feet water on it. It is called *new danger*
in the charts, a place lately discovered. We
have disabled some of our small craft, and a
fire-ship which went to Leith, by which I wrote
to you. Remember me to all, and believe me
ever with affection,

A. J. SCOTT.

March 22nd, in the evening. The frigate is
returned, and from appearances we shall fight.
I have just seen the captain, who confirms this
idea.

March 23rd, in the morning. The wind will
not permit us to pass.

We are at anchor off the Sound. Mr. Drummond is on board the frigate with all his
family. He was chargé des affaires at Copenhagen. The Kite brig goes to England with
him immediately. I fear there is a great deal
of Quixotism in this business; there is no getting any positive information of their strength.

The concluding observation in this letter
may serve to show the apprehensions excited
by Nelson's bold plan of immediate attack,
until his opinion prevailed, and the whole conduct of the expedition devolved on him. It
should be borne in mind in reading Mr. Scott's
journal, that the London was not engaged
in the action, for it had been agreed that Lord
Nelson should lead the attack, while Sir Hyde,
with a small division of the fleet, remained to
cover the retreat of the disabled ships, and
when the latter would have advanced to assist

Nelson's squadron, which had got entangled on the shoals, he was altogether prevented doing so by contrary wind and currents. It is commonly stated, that during the course of the battle Sir Hyde Parker hoisted the signal of recall, and that Nelson putting his glass to his blind eye declared he could not see it, and therefore virtually disobeyed orders. Mr. Scott's simple version of the circumstance is, that it had been arranged between the admirals, that should it appear that the ships which were engaged were suffering too severely, the signal for retreat should be made, to give Lord Nelson the option of retiring, if he thought fit.

March 29, Sunday. We still remain off the mouth of the Sound, but have approached nearer to Cronenberg, and have had some communication by a flag of truce with the Governor.

Monday, 30. Nothing more interesting, but that we are nearer the fairway between the Danish and Swedish shores. Are under sail,

and shall in a few moments pass the famous
castle, from whence they now keep up an
immense fire, although, apparently, not a shot
reaches the ships they fire at.

Monday, P.M. At anchor at Copenhagen.
Lord Nelson and Sir Hyde are now concerting
a plan of attack. They reconnoitred the
enemy's position in the Amazon. They were
warmly fired at, but needlessly, as the shot did
not reach the ship.

March 31. The admirals are employed in
arranging the mode of attack, on board the
Elephant.

April 1. Lord Nelson, with twelve ships
of the line, has anchored to the southward of
the enemy's line.

April 2. The squadron got under weigh to
attack the enemy; about twenty minutes before
eleven our ships opened their fire: the battle
lasted four hours, when the whole line, from
the southernmost end down to the Crowns, was
completely destroyed or taken.

April 3. A flag of truce is flying between us and the Danes.

April 4. The flag of truce flying. Pour parlers going on between messengers from Count Bernestoff and Sir Hyde, but nothing decisive. In the mean time wè continue repairing our ships, and getting every thing in order.

April 5. We have destroyed several of the prizes. Every thing proceeds as before. Hancock is appointed to the Cruiser, Boys to the Harpy, Maples to the Otter, &c. &c.

April 6. The Parliamentaire still in force. Lord Nelson has had a conference with the Prince. Otway goes to England with the despatches.

April 7. General Walterstorff and Adjutant-General Lindholm have had several conferences with the Prince; and to-morrow, Lord Nelson and Colonel Stewart are to go on shore, and treat about an armistice.

April 8. Went on shore as Secretary to the Legation; was presented to the Crown Prince.

After five hours *pour et contre parler* with
General Walterstorff and Adjutant-General
Lindholm, we agreed upon the heads of an
armistice. Dined with the Crown Prince, the
Prince Augustenbourg; the Crown Prince's
brother-in-law was there, as also the Prince
of Wirtemberg.

April 9. General Walterstorff and Adjutant-
General Lindholm came on board. Another
armistice was signed and sealed—after which
Lord Nelson took it ashore for the ratification
of the Crown Prince.

April 10. Nothing particular happened. No
one allowed to go on shore.

Slight as Mr. Scott's mention is, of his being
selected to go on shore as Secretary to the
Legation, it was nevertheless an office which
conferred the greatest honour upon him; since
for the fulfilment of it no ordinary abilities
were required.. It was not merely a linguist
that was wanted, but a diplomatist of skill and
tact, and experienced in the negociation of

E

delicate public business. Lord Nelson feeling
this, and appreciating, as he had the peculiar
faculty of doing, the exact qualifications of all
about him, and how to employ them to the
most advantage, fixed at once upon his old
acquaintance, Mr. Scott, for the occasion, and
applied to Sir Hyde Parker for his assistance.
Thus it happened that Mr. Scott was employed
in the arrangement of the celebrated Convention at Copenhagen, the articles of which were
drawn up by him; and so highly did Nelson
value this service, that his lordship urged him
to subscribe it with his name as the secretary;
and told him, when he modestly declined doing
so, that he would live to repent it; which
proved true. The arrangement of the articles
of this armistice had indeed required the most
delicate management; for whilst Denmark
was detached from the northern confederacy,
neither was her honour as a nation compro-
mised, nor was she exposed to the hostility of
Russia; and Lord Nelson always considered

that what Mr. Scott did in this matter, together with his zeal and ability in carrying on the correspondence with Denmark, Sweden, and Russia, both before and after signing the convention, were grounds for public reward, and stated them as such in a subsequent testimonial.

With reference also to these services, Admiral Sir Robert W. Otway, Bart., who had been captain of the Royal George, and was now on board the London, says, that Scott "maintained a correspondence with great honour and credit to himself, with the Crown Prince of Denmark; and that he acted as the confidential friend and adviser of both Sir Hyde Parker and Lord Nelson."

Despatches were received on the 22nd of April from the Russian ambassador at Copenhagen, which gave the Commander-in-chief every hope of a speedy peace with Russia. They announced the death of Paul and succession of Alexander, and the conciliating dis-

position which the new emperor instantly
manifested towards England. This checked
the course of the fleet towards Revel, and led to
communications with St. Petersburgh, to which
place Mr. Scott was very desirous of being
sent. He could not, however, persuade Sir H.
Parker to spare him; but this did not deter
his ardent mind from prosecuting the study of
the Russian language.

April 24. In the evening, anchored in Kioge
Bay. Wrote two letters to England—one for
my uncle; also I have written out a song for
Lady Lavington. Lord Nelson has invited me
to dinner on Sunday, and asked me to preach.
Captain Otway has arrived from England.

April 26. I have given the people a sermon
on board the St. George. St. Emma's day!

May 1. I have spent the whole day with
Lord Nelson, on board the St. George. He
has been ill.

May 5. Got up at two o'clock. The admiral
is ordered to England. Colonel Stewart is

come from thence. Taken leave and left the fleet.

Mr. Scott did not part from Lord Nelson without being pressed to remain in his ship, instead of returning with Sir Hyde Parker, who was just recalled; but gratifying as the invitation was to his feelings, he nevertheless declined it; stating his repugnance to quit his old friend and patron at such a moment. "He could not bear," he said, "to leave the old admiral at the very time, when he stood most in need of his company." Lord Nelson was the man of all others who could duly appreciate such conduct. It raised Mr. Scott in his estimation, by the display of sentiments which accorded with the generous warmth of his own noble heart; and he exacted a promise that he would join him as soon as he could leave Sir Hyde with satisfaction to himself.

After his return from the Baltic, he spent the remainder of the year 1801 in the society of his friends in England. He passed much of

the time in Hampshire, at Spring Hill with
Admiral Scott, at Wickham with Mr. Thomas,
and at Portsmouth with his general naval
acquaintance there. In London he was
dining out every day; and when Lord Nelson
returned on the peace of Amiens, he was very
frequently with him, both in London and at
Merton.

Anxious in any way to evince his regard for
Mr. Scott, Lord Nelson drew up the following
certificate, addressed to the Governors of the
Charter-house, with a view to its influencing
them to grant him preferment.

"Merton, Dec. 28, 1801.

"These are to certify that I have known
the Rev. A. J. Scott, from the year 1793, as a
Chaplain in the Navy, and from what I have
had the pleasure of knowing of him, and from
all I have heard, I can testify that he is a
clergyman of the greatest respectability; and
when I was in the Baltic, Mr. Scott upon va-

rious occasions, in interpreting foreign letters, was of the greatest service, and I beg leave to recommend him to the Governors of the Charter-house.

NELSON AND BRONTE.

Rt. Hon. the Governors of the Charter-house.

CHAPTER V.

Goes out to West Indies—Sir John Duckworth—made chaplain to the Leviathan—visits General Le Clerc—is struck by
lightning and wounded—presented to Southminster—Returns
to England.

THE year 1801 passed, when news from Jamaica, that Mr. Scott's living of St. John's,
was about to be given away, called for his
immediate return thither. It was with a heavy
heart—(" I am very unhappy," are his words,)
that he turned his back on England this time—
unlike the animation with which he usually
set out on any new expedition. Others have
been noticed to feel this kind of reluctance
for undertakings which have ended disastrously,
and somehow on this occasion, a shadow hung
upon Scott's spirits, when at the end of Ja-

nuary, 1802, he went on board the Téméraire,
at St. Helen's, for his passage out. Having
touched at Barbadoes and Martinique, they
reached Port Royal, on the 5th of April. Mr.
Scott's arrival was hailed with much pleasure
by his old Jamaica friends, and by the renewal
of hospitalities, which seem to have kindled
wherever he alighted. He immediately received
attentions from Admiral Sir John Duckworth,
who had succeeded Lord Hugh Seymour in
the command on the station, and in June was
appointed chaplain to his flag-ship the Leviathan.
It happened that just then, Admiral Duckworth
was in much anxiety to discover the ultimate
designs of General Le Clerc, (Buonaparte's brother-in-law,) who had for some months occupied
St. Domingo, with 20,000 French troops, besides a large naval armament. The ostensible
reason for this great expedition, was the recovery of that fine colony from the Blacks under
the ill-fated Toussaint. The force, however,
was too extensive, and the perfidy of the French

government too well established, not to render
the presence of this army, a subject of apprehension to the English Colonies, although hostilities with France were suspended.   Admiral
Duckworth, therefore, finding in Mr. Scott, in
addition to his'perfect knowledge of the French
language, and dexterity in negociation, the
talent of rendering himself agreeable in society,
and to those with whom he had to deal, requested him as a personal favour to embark
in the Topaz frigate, which he would send with
him to St. Domingo, for the avowed object of
complimenting General Le Clerc, on his presence
in the West Indies, but instructing him to find
out in conversation with the French officers,
what was really intended by so large a force.
Mr. Scott cheerfully undertook the mission,
and sailed in the Topaz, with Captain Macna-
mara.*   They arrived at Cape François, on the
13th July, and on the 15th, Mr. Scott visited

* Afterwards notorious from having been tried for killing
Col. Montgomery in a duel.

General Le Clerc in the country, and was graciously entertained by him at dinner.   At this
dinner party, a conversation took place between
Madame Le Clerc and Mr. Scott, which was
not a little characteristic of the insolent as-
sumption of the usurping family.   Madame
Le Clerc having led the conversation to the
superior prosperity and splendour of France,
under her brother's government; the flou-
rishing state of arts, commerce and manufac-
tures; at length drew his attention to an
exquisitely beautiful set of China that was
on the table, instancing it as a specimen of
the perfection to which every thing was carried
under the new régime.   Mr. Scott took up
the plate that was before him, as if to examine
it carefully, and while expressing his excessive
admiration of its merits, turned it quietly over
and discovered the mark underneath, which
was the head of the unhappy Marie Antoinette.
" What is this?" said he, holding up the plate
and scrutinizing it yet more closely.   " Ah !"

he added, " now I see, it is the portrait of the
Queen of France !"   Every one was silent,
for every one present knew what Mr. Scott
also had been well aware of, that the china
was of a peculiar pattern and manufacture,
which had been appropriated especially to the
use of Marie Antoinette.   But so inexplicable
was Mr. Scott's manner that Pauline was utterly
unable to detect whether his remark had been
an unconscious or intentional reprimand, so
she laughed it off with the easy assurance of a
Frenchwoman, and immediately changed the
conversation.   It may be conjectured that the
vision this allusion brought before her of her
family's having succeeded to the glory of regal
power, was not altogether unacceptable to the
beautiful Pauline ; and that, in that point of
view, her vanity almost extracted from the
reproof, a compliment to her triumphant situation.

A very few days' observation satisfied Mr.
Scott, that however suspicious might be the

real views of the French, the climate was doing its fell work in thinning their ranks, and dis- organizing their army, and that no immediate danger to the security of the British Colonies need be apprehended. He was therefore re- turning to Jamaica, in the frigate, when on the passage, the ship soon after midnight, was struck by lightning in a severe thunderstorm. The electric fluid rent the mizenmast, killing and wounding fourteen men, and descending into the Captain's cabin, in which Mr. Scott was sleeping, communicated with some spare cartridges and powder horns, which lay on a shelf immediately over his head. By this means he sustained a double shock, the electric fluid struck his hand and arm, passing along the bell wire, with which they were in contact, and the gunpowder exploding at the same time knocked out some of his front teeth, and dreadfully lacerated his mouth and jaw. The lightning also melted the hooks to which the hammock was slung, and he fell to the ground,

receiving a violent concussion of the brain.
His cabin was found in flames, himself a sheet
of fire, and he was. taken up senseless and
apparently not likely to live. On landing, he
was lodged in a convent, at Kingston, and by
the excellent skill of Dr. Blair, physician to
the fleet in the West Indies, he soon recovered
from his external injuries; but one side of his
body was paralyzed for a length of time—his
sight, hearing, and the powers of his mind
were also impaired—the last so much so as to
cause general apprehension that he would never
regain them; and the nervous system was so
completely shattered by the accident, that he
suffered from it for the remainder of his life.
It was some consolation in the midst of this
distress, and the anxiety consequent upon the
suspension of his Jamaica living, to receive
news from England, that the Governors of the
Charter-house, had presented him to the Vicarage of Southminster, in Essex. " August 18,
Received my letters. I am Vicar of South-

minster;" is the languid notice in his diary of
this event.

TO THE REV. G. A. THOMAS,

Rectory, Wickham, Hants.

Jamaica, Sept. 4, 1804.

MY DEAR THOMAS,—I am infinitely better
than ever I expected to be; in short, if the
affliction of my side quits me, which the doctors
promise, and the sensations in my head, which
come on now less frequently, do not incapaci-
tate me, I shall do very well. My face, except
the loss of two teeth, will be as beautiful
as ever, for the scars they assure me will
vanish. Nothing afflicts me but the idea
that my memory is impaired. It is true my
living was given away by the Governor, but
most illegally, and in opposition to additional
leave of absence granted by himself, and when
of course, there was no avoidance. I have held
silent merely to establish an interest with him
for Mr. Harper, who, I think, with a living

in this country, would soon acquire a large
fortune. I am uncommonly well this morning.
I, tried a carriage yesterday, but it would
not do. I cannot bear loud talking, and
my nerves are as delicate as yours. Sir J.
Duckworth writes to the Bishop of London an
account of the accident which has prevented
me from getting to England in time. I shall
be with you in the first ship, which I believe
will be either the Chichester store-ship, or
Ganges, 74. I feel much for my poor uncle,
and wish you could get him out a little. The
Charter-house passed a vote for building a
house at Southminster; if it is not yet done,
I will endeavour to persuade him to go there
with me and direct. This is my uncle's hobby-
horse; and I suppose the Charity having
ordered the building of one at its expense, to a
certain extent, will have no objection to my
plan, if within bounds. In the summer, you
might, as I do not often get a living, go to
Southend, and see me properly installed.

Southend is a watering-place, close to my parish. I mention this, in case my house should not be built time enough to receive you. I expect to get three-and-sixpence a-day, half-pay, as chaplain in the navy, which will help me on in furnishing it. The doctors wish me to go to Bath, and drink the waters; but I do not like to quit the sea-side, as I feel myself nearer England. However, as soon as I can travel, I must go there, if only for a week. The water is exactly the same as that of Bath in England; and bathing-places are established, &c. If a ship sails within a month I may yet save the lapse; but I trust, considering all things, and my unfortunate situation, no advantage will be taken of it, if I am too late. Pray make every inquiry you can about the place, and the cheapest and best mode of sending my books from Southampton thither. I have a number of pursuits warm in my imagination, and I pray to God I may not in England be subject to the head fits I now am.

You are probably yet to know that I have received two shocks at the same time; one electric, and the other from the explosion of the powder horns. I have walked out several times slowly, but it brings on a very great nervous agitation. When I am safe at South-minster, I mean to exclaim—

Inveni portum, spes et fortuna, &c.

And over my door shall be written—

Πολλων δ'ανθρωπων ιδεν αστεα, και νοον εγνω,
Πολλα δ' ογ' ενπουτω παθεν αλγεα.

I would have you know, that I esteem Greek before any language; but I cannot help think-ing the English inferior to the Italian. What you observe about our authors is not a fair statement; but of this when we meet.

My dear Mrs. Thomas,—I most heartily thank you for your kind letter, but I cannot engage to answer it now; but I hope by the end of November to do it in person. I am

fixed to go in the next man-of-war, notwithstanding the winter months. Indeed, if possible, I would set off immediately in the packet,
but there are no accommodations for me in it;
and the noise would hurt me in so small a
vessel, where no quiet place is to be found.
I never mean to marry for love, you must
know, but I desire you will look out for me.
Inquire how fares it with Miss North—I mean
Lucy, not the youngest; but Mr. Thomas is
seldom accurate in these matters. I hope you
will keep the anniversary of the dance at the
rectory, on the 5th of October, and that the
leg of the table will not be forgotten. I suppose the bishop also will be there. Remember
me to all. I must conclude,

A. J. Scott.

I do not leave off because I am tired, for I
neither see company, nor go out, nor read,
nor write, except what you see in England of
my scrawl. I earnestly and urgently wish to

leave this island, but what can I do? My
baggage was already on board the Syren frigate,
when illness prevented my departure by a sudden strange attack. I long to behold the last
moment of remaining here—Νωστησας δ'επειτα
φιλην εις πατριδα γαιαν—ask Mr. Thomas.

My dear Thomas, remember me to the children, Mr. Ford, the captain and Emma; do not
forget the anniversary ball to the bishop and
Garnier family, even if the 5th of October is
past—by the bye, everything to that family for
me and Tom Garnier.

It was not till the 7th of December that poor
Scott was able to crawl away from Jamaica in
the Cerberus frigate, and on the passage, which
was a very stormy one throughout, he had
another very narrow escape with his life. The
frigate during a heavy gale of wind which blew
for many days without intermission, obscuring
sun and sky, carrying away the mizenmast,
and doing other serious damage to the vessel,

shipped a sea which deluged his cabin, and, as
his feebleness prevented him from extricating
himself from the mosquito net of his cot, in
which he had got entangled, he certainly would
have been drowned, but for timely assistance.
Coming in sight of the coast of Ireland, they
ran into Bantry Bay for shelter, from whence
Scott was glad to escape to Southampton, with
the hope before him of further medical relief
from his painful accident, and of the quietude
of a clergyman's life in an agricultural parish.

CHAPTER VI.

Takes possession of Southminster—illness—becomes chaplain
and secretary to Lord Nelson in the Victory—Mediterranean
—duties as secretary, &c.

WE will now briefly advert to the changes that
had taken place among Mr. Scott's connexions
during his services abroad.   His mother, whom
he had always liberally assisted, although there
had been times when he could ill afford it, had
again entered the marriage state, and both his
sisters had also married.   The one, after losing
her first husband, Captain Reddall of the Royal
Navy, reunited herself to Admiral Douglas; and
the other became the wife of Mr. Harper, a
clergyman of the Church of England.   Mrs.
Scott, of Spring Hill, for whom her nephew
had always entertained much affection, had

died during the latter part of his stay in the
West Indies, and we believe that the Admiral
had been still further afflicted by the loss of
some of his children. To the relations which
were left him, Mr. Scott returned with every
hope of renewing his domestic associations
among them, and of enjoying the blessings of
a home, the value of which no man knew better
how to appreciate. After visiting his uncle
and Mr. Thomas, the old and dear friend to
whom his last letter was addressed, he came to
London for institution to his living, and hastened to Southminster to take possession. He
qualified also for a magistrate, and in all points
prepared himself for undertaking the duties of
a country clergyman's life. His warm-hearted
intentions, however, were speedily turned into
a new channel by the current of unexpected
events. On returning to London he was again
attacked by severe illness, which confined him
to his hotel. Lord Nelson, to whom he had
written from Jamaica an account of his acci-

dent, hearing that he was in town, was soon at his bedside, and was much shocked at finding him so altered in appearance, and injured in constitution, by the consequences of his wounds. He continually visited him during this attack ; and seeing that in fact he was totally unfit to undertake the duties of his parish, which was unhealthily situated in the marshes of Essex ; and, thinking that his services to his country were worthy of some professional reward, he drew up the following testimonial, which it was intended should accompany a petition to the Treasury.

" These are to certify that the Rev. Mr. Scott was employed by me in arrangement of the Convention at Copenhagen, and Mr. Scott upon every occasion showed his readiness and ability in translating French and German papers, and as he has suffered by being employed in the public service by Sir J. T. Duckworth, I really think him a very proper object for the consideration of government.

" I have such a high opinion of Mr. Scott's ability and honour, that, if he is well enough, I should feel happy, on being appointed to a foreign command, to have him as my foreign secretary, and to be confidentially employed with business to foreign ministers.

" NELSON AND BRONTE."

Little did Lord Nelson think, while penning this memorial, in how short a time he would have an opportunity of proving the sincerity of his expressions! Within a few days afterwards the peace of Amiens was dissolved, war was declared anew with France, and Lord Nelson, at a day's notice, was put in command of the Mediterranean fleet, with unusual powers. He instantly desired Mr. Scott to accompany him as chaplain, and his foreign and confidential secretary, and overruled every conscientious scruple that could suggest itself to his friend's mind. His inability to perform his duties at Southminster—the benefit he would derive from

the salubrious climate of the Mediterranean—
the probability of only a short absence, were
all made apparent, and, as there was no time
for explanations or apologies, Lord Nelson undertook himself to exonerate him to the Bishop
of London. Thus was Mr. Scott prevailed
upon, " though very ill," to comply with Lord
Nelson's wishes, and, as he accepted employment, it was not judged proper to present the
memorial. It was therefore withheld, (to quote
Dr. Scott's own words,) " under the impression
that, if presented, a pecuniary remuneration
would have been the result, whereas, by waiting, and adding further services, he might rise
in his profession."

Nothing could exceed the promptitude with
which Lord Nelson undertook his new command. It was only on the 16th of May, that
a message from the king announced to both
houses of parliament the necessity of immediate
war with France, and, on the 17th, the commander-in-chief was at Portsmouth, ready to

embark. His secretary left town at eleven o'clock at night on the 16th, and, upon his arrival at Southampton, prepared, (as the diary records,) some books to take with him in his intended voyage with Lord Nelson.

May 18, Wednesday. Set off for Wickham, with my cousins. Dined there, and at night arrived at Portsmouth with Thomas. Immediately made my bow to Lord Nelson, and presented Mr. Thomas to him, who was very proud of that honour.

May 19, Thursday. Presented Thomas to Lady Saxton, after which he left me, and returned to Wickham. Dined at the commissioner's.

May 20. Came on board the Amphion— soon after breakfast sailed in company with the Victory.

May 21. Took the Orion, a Dutch ship, sailing down Channel, from Surinam bound to the Texel.

May 22. Made Ushant.

May 23. Got to the rendezvous of the fleet. Lord Nelson, Mrs. Elliot, &c. came on board.

May 24. Fair wind, proceeding on our course.

May 25. Saw Cape Ortegal.

May 26. Wind contrary—saw a whale.

May 27. Wind contrary—saw Island Cisarga.

May 28. Heavy sea—wind contrary.

May 29, Whitsunday. No prayers—wind contrary—heavy sea and rain.

May 30, Monday. Nota Bene. Read during the last week, Les Femmes, leur condition, et leur influence dans l'ordre social. Wind contrary, but at 12 o'clock found the ship to be to the southward of Cape Finisterre.

May 31. Very calm in the morning—began to read Chrysal yesterday, and some prose essays of W. Shenstone, on Men and Manners, which I do not recollect ever to have seen before. Nota Bene. Read also last week Borzacchini's Italian Grammar—the 6th vol. of Sevigné's Letters in hand. *Pride*, a good subject for a sermon, and never yet I believe, properly

argued against from the pulpit. It is usually
said, that, considering the infirmities of our
nature, &c. &c., Pride was not made for man;
but man is not proud as a species, but as an
individual; not as comparing himself with other
beings, but with his fellow creatures. Finished
Shenstone's Essays in the afternoon—the wind
favourable and increasing—several spermaceti
whales passed by this evening.

June 1. The wind still favourable, but not
strong—carrying us about three miles an hour.
Charity is a disposition to *think* well, and *do*
well to all human beings without partiality, prejudice, or respect to any other motive than this
universal duty; giving of alms being only one,
and that perhaps the meanest effect of it. The
wind stronger before dinner.

June 2. Very early in the morning saw two
ships, one like a frigate, at the same time being
in sight of the Rock of Lisbon—wind favourable
and going eight knots—passed at nine o'clock
in the evening Cape St. Vincent.

June 3. Passed Cape Trafalgar—took a French brig from Guadaloupe to Marseilles, and anchored in the evening at Gibraltar. Wrote several letters.

June 4. King's birthday—saluted garrison, Portuguese admiral, and his majesty—remained on board from illness—quitted Gibraltar at three o'clock in the afternoon—gave chase in company with the Maidstone frigate, to a ship and a brig in Tetuan Bay—cleared for action —passed Ceuta, which, with the fortifications, appeared in a beautiful point of view—answered the chase signal, which proved to be the Tour-terelle, and bore up for Malta.

June 5, Trinity Sunday. Took a Dutch brig from Sette in Languedoc to Amsterdam. About an hour after took a French brig called Le Silvain, bound from Sette to St. Malo.

June 6. Continued our course with a fair wind, speaking several vessels. In company still with the Maidstone.

June 7. The wind contrary—made the

African shore, and continued to work up in shore.

June 8. Read Veneroni's Grammar, which, indeed, has been in hand for several days past, as well as Borzacchini's—read Dr. Moore's Life of Smollett.

So far Mr. Scott's journal had been kept in English, on the 9th of June, it commences in Italian, with occasional entries in German. We have evidences, from scattered memoranda during the previous month, of constant close study of the Italian language and idioms, with the aid of *three* Italian Grammars, which prove how accurately he studied.

June 9. I have read nothing to day but Veneroni's and Borzacchini's Grammars. The wind, though contrary in the morning, became fair in the evening, and blew fresh at night.

June 10. The wind favours us much—we see the coast of Mauritania round Algiers—wrote to Mr. Thomas; this evening the wind fell a little—began Zotti's Grammar.

June 11. The ambassador to the court of Naples set out in the Maidstone frigate. We are near the mountains of Mauritania.

June 12, first Sunday after Trinity. Eclectism—prayers and sermon, " God who at sundry times and in divers places." The wind not good.

June 13. Read the day before yesterday, the Merope of Maffei, and the Demofoonte of Metastasio. Began the Lettres de Cachet of Mirabeau—saw a great number of fishing boats employed in the coral fishery—supposed Corsicans and Sardinians, who keep all together, in order to repel the Turks.

June 14. Passed Galita early in the morning —saw a large Moorish town—passed by Zembra, a large rock in the Bay of Tunis—towards night passed Pantalleria, a small island belonging to Naples, to which criminals are banished.

June 15. Made the island of Gozo—then Commino and Malta, in the port of which we arrived. Sir Alexander Ball is come on board

to pay his respects to my Lord Nelson. Went
on shore with my Lord to pay a visit to General Villette, and to the wife of General Bickerton, and then, having drunk tea at Lady Ball's,
we returned on board.

June 16. Having finished my work and duty,
I went ashore with Captain Elliot, and Sir A.
Ball, who has had the politeness to show us the
Arsenal, sending one of his officers to accompany us. We found it really a beautiful sight.
The white arms of very many grand masters,
officers, and soldiers; muskets after the modern
fashion, and many arms after the ancient.
Among these, there was a cannon of hard lea-
ther, lined with brass. In the same room there
were two sceptres of Turkish emperors, killed
or made prisoners, I know not where, and many
Turkish arms. Leaving the Armoury, we proceeded to a bookseller's, where I bought
" Malta Illustrata;" and, in a neighbouring
shop, the Philosophy of Buffon, in 30 volumes.
A Maltese, native of Valetta, has constituted

himself my servant; his name is Pietro. Having seen the fortifications, and, being wearied with so much walking about, I repaired on board. At half past three, I accompanied the Admiral to the house of Sir Alexander Ball, where he received the visits of the magistrates, of some of the clergy, and a Mameluke of rank and noble presence. The hilt of his sword was covered with diamonds. After dining with General Villette we went to see the Church of St. Giovanni; from thence in calashes to the Botanical Garden, and to the country houses of Generals Villette and Okes. That of the former is a very delightful villa, and in former times belonged to the Family of Rohan. We returned on board just as they were beginning to illuminate the city, in honour of Lord Nelson.

This was the last occasion of Lord Nelson going on shore for a period of very nearly two years.

They sailed from Malta the next day, and

coasting by Sicily, proceeded northward through the Straits of Messina. Mr. Scott was still in the Amphion. His notes merely enumerate the beautiful features of the scenery by which they passed. Ætna and Stromboli, with the coast of Calabria, at one view. Then Capri Ischia, Baiæ, the Bay of Naples, the fortress of St. Elmo, with Vesuvius in the distance. Such are the pictures he draws, and the effect of them, with the soothing influence of a Mediterranean sea and sky in fine weather, evidently much allayed the nervous irritation of his frame. " Proceed due on in the course of virtue," is a moral entry in his diary of this date, " and like the sea which now surrounds us, never know retiring ebb." They soon came up with the fleet in the gulf of Genoa, when Mr. Scott went on board the Victory, and it may be considered that the two most arduous and eventful years of his life then fairly commenced. Lord Nelson took his station immediately off Toulon, where the difficulties he had to en-

counter were of so complicated and harassing
a nature, and required so much untiring pa-
tience and watchfulness, that they gave full
and anxious employment, not only to himself,
but to all who were in his confidential service.
We need only consider that on every side of
the fleet was either avowed enmity, or a neutrality so ill observed, owing to the active
interference of Buonaparte's emissaries in every
quarter, that it was more mischievous and irri-
tating than even direct war; and we shall perceive that the Admiral's anxious temperament
could have enjoyed little rest, or permitted it
to others, The French fleet was to be
blockaded in port, or forced to battle if they
put to sea; Naples, Sicily, Sardinia, and Spain,
were to be preserved, if possible, from the
overspreading tyranny of Buonaparte, and of
these, Naples was already almost in the hands
of the French; the south of Italy was occupied
by their troops; Sardinia and Sicily were
threatened with invasion; and Spain was every

day becoming more faithless to her neutrality.
To combat all these difficulties, Lord Nelson
had, it is true, every facility afforded him by
Government which the situation admitted of.
He was sent out with a very numerous fleet, and
intrusted with almost unlimited powers. Every
English ambassador, envoy, or consul in the
Mediterranean, was directed to forward to him
duplicate despatches, and to receive and obey all
orders from him. Could the struggle have been
brought to the issue of arms, Nelson's triumph
would not in all probability have been long
delayed, but, as it was, he was unable to force
the enemy to fight, and had therefore no resource but to oppose their undermining policy
with weapons of diplomacy, which he well knew
how to use, although it was a sore and vexa-
tious trial to his active spirit to be confined to
such a comparatively inglorious warfare. Arduous and ungrateful as the task was to his
feelings, Lord Nelson sat down to it with the
heart of a hero, trusting, as he expressed it in a

letter to the Duc de Genevois, Viceroy of Sardinia, " that the blessing of a just God would
accompany his efforts, and that he should be
able to defeat the cunning of the Corsican
tyrant."

In confirmation (were such indeed wanting)
of the anxious zeal of Nelson, in the fulfilment
of the great charge intrusted to him,—the
maintenance of the neutrality, and the protection of the Mediterranean states, (especially
that state, from its resources, its position, and
the favourable dispositions of its rulers, of all
the most important to us,) in proof, too, of the
clear-sightedness of his own great political
views, we here inserta portion of this illustrious man's correspondence with the Queen
of Naples :—

TO THE QUEEN OF NAPLES.

Off Toulon, July 26, 1803.

MADAM,—The first great object which is
always nearest my heart, is the safety of the

persons of your Majesties, and of all the royal family. The second, so far as it is in my power, is that of the kingdom of Naples, which is a very difficult affair.

If your Majesty were to act with all the circumspection in your power, either the French would feel themselves offended, or what is worse, if possible, their assistance would be given by force to the King, for the *preservation* of Sicily. The great wisdom of your Majesty, will know all that I could allege upon this subject. I shall therefore only say, that if Sicily is lost, Europe will blame the councils of his Sicilian Majesty and Lord Nelson, for having been so weak as to pay attention to, or credit what is reported by the agents of the present French government.

I have written to the English government, declaring fully the unhappy position of the kingdom of Naples ; regretting the orders given for the return of the army of Egypt, and setting forth with energy the necessity for sending troops, not only to assist in the defence of Sicily, but in sufficient numbers to place garrisons in Gaeta, in the castles of Naples, if it should be expedient, and to send a body of men into Calabria, to support the loyal and brave inhabitants of that country of mountains, in case the French should be too imperious in their demands.

His Excellency, Mr. Elliot, will inform your Majesty of the difficulty I have in leaving a ship of the line at Naples, considering the present state of the enemy's fleet at Toulon; but I will never permit my personal feelings to weigh against the sacred interest, which I shall always take in the safety and well-being of your Majesties, and of all the royal family; and I assure your Majesty, that I am always

Your most devoted and faithful servant,

NELSON AND BRONTE.

TO THE QUEEN OF NAPLES.

Victory, Dec. 29, 1803.

MADAM,—Yesterday evening I had the honour of receiving your Majesty's gracious and flattering letter of the 10th December; and it is only possible for me to repeat my assurances, that my orders for the safety of the Two Sicilies, will be always exactly executed, and to this end my whole soul goes in unison with my orders. The Gibraltar shall not be sent away, for I would rather fight twice our number of forces, than risk for a moment the seeing your royal person and family fall into the hands of the French. I see no hope of a permanent peace for Europe, during the life of Buonaparte. I ardently wish, therefore, that it would please God to take him from the world.

Your Majesty's letter to my dear and good Lady Hamilton, shall set out by the first opportunity. Her attachment to your Majesty is as lively as ever. Her heart is incapable of the slightest change; and whether in prosperity or in adversity, she is always your devoted servant; and such, permit me to say, remains your faithful

NELSON AND BRONTE.

I beg to be allowed to present my humble respects to the Princesses, and to Prince Leopold.

TO THE QUEEN OF NAPLES.

Victory, 10th July, 1804.

MADAM,—I have been honoured by your Majesty's gracious and condescending letter of June 28th. I have no other reply to make to such flattering expressions of confidence, than to offer my most devoted thanks, and my assurances of always studying to merit your Majesty's favourable sentiments, and those of my benefactor, the King.

It would be presumptuous on my part to

venture to speak of political matters in a letter
to your Majesty; but I cannot help wishing
that Europe was like a handful of rods against
France. If it be proper to give way to the
times—let us temporise : if to make war—let
us all make it. On this principle, I could
have wished that Russia had avoided war,
unless she had been joined by Austria. Then,
acting honourably side by side, there would
have been some hope from such a coalition.

If Russia sends men and vessels to the
Ionian republic, and into the Morea only, I
have no hesitation in saying, that she compro-
mises Naples much more, than if she had, for
the moment, bent to the storm. At least
50,000 troops (it should be 100,000) are necessary to answer for the safety of Italy. To
say the truth, I do not believe we had in the
last war, and according to all appearance, we
shall not have in the present one either, plans,
of a sufficiently grand scale, to force France
to keep within her proper limits. Small

measures produce only small results. I dare
not let my pen run on. The intelligent mind
of your Majesty will readily comprehend the
great things which might be effected in the
Mediterranean. On this side Buonaparte is
the most vulnerable. It is from here that it
would be most easy to mortify his pride, and
so far humble him, as to make him accept
reasonable conditions of peace. I entreat your
Majesty's pardon for having expressed my
sentiments with such boldness.

Mr. Elliot has informed me by writing, of
what your Majesty wished to say on the subject of writing to the minister, respecting the
pension for your Emma. Poor Sir William
Hamilton believed that it would have been
granted, or it would have been unpardonable
in him to have left his widow with so little
means. Your Majesty well knows, that it was
her capacity and conduct which sustained his
diplomatic character, during the last years in
which he was at Naples. It is unnecessary

for me to speak more of it. It only remains
for me—begging pardon for having occupied
your Majesty's time so long—to subscribe
myself

Your Majesty's faithful and devoted servant,

NELSON AND BRONTE.

From what has been shown, it will easily be
imagined that the business to be transacted
had become immense. The histories of Nelson
describe him as at this time, having often full
employment for both his English and foreign
secretaries, and Dr. Scott's diaries, brief as
they are, record his own days of unremitting
labour, accompanied sometimes with the obser·
vation, "I have had no time to read." The
examination of all papers and letters found on
board the prizes, as well as of the captains of
the vessels, was one of his occupations, and the
utmost resources of his readiness in languages,
were on some of these occasions called upon,

as the vessels came from almost every quarter of the civilized globe. The journal of a few days in July, 1803, may be amusing as a specimen of his labours, and we give it in his own Italian.

"Lunedi ai 18 di Luglio, 1803. Tutta la settimana passata son stato moltissimo occupato colle lettere venute dal Mare nero. Consiglio di Guerra si teneva oggi.

Martedì ai 19. Sempre occupato colle lettere.

Mercoledì ai 20. Colle lettere d' Adrianopoli occupato.

Giovedì ai 21. Occupatissimo con quelle di Constantinopoli, e della Canée.

Venerdì ai 22. Colle lettere di Smirne occupato.

Sabato ai 23. Come jeri moltissimo occupato con quelle sopra-mentovate lettere.

Domenica ai 24. L'ottava Domenica dopo quella della santissima Trinità, lette le preghiere.

Martedì ai 26. Sempre colle lettere occupato.

Mercoledì ai 27. Finito di leggere le lettere di Smirne.

Giovedì ai 28. Rincontrato quel Cap. Gusca —esaminatolo con due altri Capitani.

Venerdì ai 29. Mi ha dato il Cap. Elliot, due libretti italiani trovati abbordo d' un piccolissimo bastimento, jeri sera, che è stato preso ai Francesi.

Sabato ai 30. Abboccato con il Cap. Spagnuolo d'una " *chica embarcacion veniente,*" da Cadice facendo rotta per Genova, &c. &c.

It must also be mentioned that Lord Nelson made it a point of etiquette, to accompany all his original English letters to foreign courts with translations in their respective languages, and the preparing these was an office that occupied much of Dr. Scott's attention; as, besides constant communications with the royal families of Naples and Sardinia, a correspondence was carried on, at intervals, during the greater part of the blockade of Toulon, with the Dey of Algiers, the unsettled and

intricate state of affairs between that personage
and the English Government, causing Lord
Nelson a great deal of annoyance and weari-
some negotiation, as will be seen hereafter,
when we come to speak of Dr. Scott's services
on shore.

Besides the graver employments above spoken of, Dr. Scott was in the habit of reading
to his chief all the French, Italian, Spanish
and other foreign newspapers, which were sent
regularly to the fleet, and these were ran-
sacked as well for the amusement, as the information they contained. Dr. Scott had also to
wade through numberless ephemeral foreign
pamphlets, which a mind less investigating
than Lord Nelson's would have discarded as
totally unworthy of notice ; but he entertained
a persuasion that no man ever put his hand
to paper, without having some information or
theory to deliver, which he fancied was not
generally known ; and that this was worth
looking after, through all the encumbering

rubbish. His own quickness in detecting the
drift of an author was perfectly marvellous.
Two or three pages of a pamphlet were generally sufficient to put him in complete possession of the writer's object, and nothing was
too trivial for the attention of this great
man's mind, when there existed a possibility
of its being the means of obtaining information.

Day after day might be seen the admiral in
his cabin, closely employed with his secretary
over their interminable papers. They occupied
two black leathern armchairs, into the roomy
pockets of which, Scott, weary of translating,
would occasionally stuff away a score or two of
unopened private letters, found in prize ships,
although the untiring activity of Nelson
grudged leaving one such document unexa-
mined. These chairs, with an ottoman that
belongs to them, (now treasured heirlooms in
Dr. Scott's family,) formed when lashed together, a couch, on which the hero often slept,

G

those brief slumbers for which he was remark-able.

Happily for Dr. Scott, all his services were in the truest sense, labours of love. No man ever possessed, in a more remarkable degree than Lord Nelson, the power of exciting simul-taneously affection for his person, and admira-tion of his genius. Sir Pulteney Malcolm, whose extraordinary fate it had been to be intimately acquainted with Buonaparte, the Duke of Wellington, and our great naval hero, used to say, (but, perhaps, with the partiality of a sailor,) that "Nelson was the man to *love*."

Every evening Scott was with his chief, and he was constantly a guest at his table. The great regard Lord Nelson entertained for him, strengthened with acquaintance, and became especially apparent during the years 1804 and 1805. In a letter to Mr. Rose, dated May 25th, 1804, his lordship said, "the Rev. Mr. Scott desires me to present his best respects to you, and I cannot let this opportunity slip of

telling you that his abilities are of a very superior cast, and that he would be a most valuable
acquisition to any one high in office.   He lives
with me, I can therefore speak confidently of
his ability."

Nelson not only appreciated his extraordinary
talents, but his high character also, his excessive naturalness, and refinement of mind; and
seeing in him, in union with a capacity for very
difficult services, a simplicity that often put
him at disadvantage in worldly matters, it
became a common joke with him, that "the
doctor would always want somebody to take
care of him."

He spoke of him as "the doctor," for after
they became intimate in the Victory, he always
addressed him as either Doctor or Scott, although he had not yet taken his D.D. degree.

Lord Nelson was constantly studying the
characters of those whom he had about him,
and would lead them into discussions in which
he afterwards took no part, for the mere pur-

pose of drawing out their thoughts and opinions ; and even for debating the most important naval business he preferred a turn on
the quarter-deck with his captains, whom he
led by his own frankness to express themselves freely, to all the stiffness and formality
of a council of war.

In accordance with this habit, he was very
fond of conversing with Dr. Scott, being interested by the originality of his thoughts, and
the warm and enthusiastic manner in which he
delivered them, as well as by the store of information with which his indefatigable habit
of reading furnished him. We are assured by
an eye-witness, that often after dinner Lord
Nelson would amuse himself by leading the
doctor into arguments on literature, politics,
Spanish, and even naval affairs, and would
occasionally provoke from him a lecture on
navigation itself; to the great entertainment of
Admiral Murray, Captain Hardy, and other
officers present. We need hardly say, that on

board ship such things could not have happened
except under the utmost encouragement on the
part of the admiral. But Lord Nelson's manner, apart from duty, was universally kind and
even playful to all around him; an amusing
instance of which, as well as of his extreme
quickness, occurred during this cruise in the
Mediterranean.

One bright morning, when the ship was
moving about four knots an hour through a
very smooth sea, everything on board being
orderly and quiet, there was a sudden cry of
"a man overboard!" A midshipman, named
Flinn, a good draughtsman, who had been
sitting on deck comfortably sketching, started
at the cry, and looking over the side of the
ship, saw his own servant, who was no swimmer,
floundering in the sea. Before Flinn's jacket
could be off, the captain of marines had
thrown the man a chair through the port-hole
in the wardroom, to keep him floating, and in
the next instant Flinn had flung himself over-

board and was swimming to the rescue. The
admiral having witnessed the whole affair from
the quarter-deck, was highly delighted with the
scene, and when the party, chair and all, had
been hauled upon deck, he called Mr. Flinn,
praised his conduct, and made him lieutenant
on the spot. A loud huzza from the midshipmen, whom the incident had collected on deck,
and who were throwing up their hats in honour
of Flinn's good fortune, arrested Lord Nelson's
attention. There was something significant in
the tone of their cheer which he immediately
recognised, and putting up his hand for silence,
and leaning over to the crowd of middies, he
said, with a good-natured smile on his face,
" Stop, young gentlemen ! Mr. Flinn has done
a gallant thing to-day—and he has done many
gallant things before—for which he has got his
reward, but mind ! *I'll have no more making
lieutenants for servants falling overboard.*"

In further proof of his general kindness of
heart, it may be mentioned that the Victory

had an unusual number of midshipmen in her, in consequence of Lord Nelson complying with the, request of parents that their sons should sail with him, and he frequently invited them to his table, and treated them universally with the greatest affability and good-nature.

CHAPTER VII.

Missions into Spain, Sardinia—Magnon—Barcelona sale—mission to Algiers, Sicily, Naples—journal—pursuit of the
French to the West Indies—and return home.

ALTHOUGH Dr. Scott's health improved much
after he left England, the shock his nervous
system had sustained made him peculiarly sensible of the irksome confinement of shipboard,
on which account it was thought good for the
general relief of his mind, that he should have
the opportunity of enjoying frequent change of
scene; and it was a fortunate circumstance,
that what was so much for his benefit, was also
made to contribute materially to the public
good; for the use derived from his abilities as
an agent on shore, was even greater than from
his employment as foreign secretary. As a

confidential agent he was exactly the man required—full of observation—agreeable where-
ever he went—able to understand all he heard
and saw—whilst his condition as an invalid, and
his pursuits as a scholar, facilitated his opportunities. Often, therefore, as he was sent into Spain,
to Naples, &c. &c., *apparently* for his pleasure or
for the benefit of his health, it was never without
some special purpose. The object of those missions was known to himself and the admiral
alone- at the time they occurred, the business
being kept so strictly secret that there is no
mention even in the diary, of what took place
on any one occasion; a precaution which may
also have been dictated by common prudence,
as he was constantly liable to fall into the
hands of the French faction. Happily, however, no misfortune of this kind ever befell him ;
but there can be no doubt that the risks he
ran were considerable, and it is most interesting to record what we have been assured of by
an eye-witness, that when Dr. Scott was ab-

sent on these services, Lord Nelson was in a
state of the most restless uneasiness and anxiety on his account; and when the few days'
absence was over, "was always more pleased to
see Dr. Scott safe back, than at the success of
his missions." It may be stated generally of
his employments in Spain, that he was gaining
information throughout Catalonia, (which, as
a province adjoining France, was overrun by
French influence,) and establishing every possible quick means of communication between
Madrid, Barcelona, and the fleet. Some of his
visits on shore in Sardinia had, however, another most important object, of which mention
must now be made. The long time the fleet
occupied one station rendered the victualling
of the ships a matter of great difficulty, watched
as they were from every coast, by a powerful
enemy who overawed any tendency in the neutral countries to assist them. To return southward—to Malta for instance—would have been
to give up the Toulon fleet, and forsake the

defence of Naples. It was, therefore, highly
necessary to find harbour and provisions at
some point, so situated as to enable them at
the same time to maintain a close observation
of the enemy. For this purpose, no place was
more convenient than the island of Sardinia,
which, at both extremities, had harbourage for
any number of ships. The Gulf of Palmas at
the south offered not only safe and commodious
anchorage, but great facilities also for obtaining
supplies; and, at the north point, was the group
of the Maddalene Islands, which, with the
main land, offered several secure harbours, capable of containing fleets, and affording ingress
and egress with any winds.

To Sardinia, therefore, Lord Nelson chiefly
trusted for the victualling of his ships, and his
first object was to do away, if possible, the im-
pediments that arose from the neutrality to
which her government was pledged; in the
accomplishment of which point Dr. Scott's
services were invaluable—" He was," to use

the words of a distinguished living admiral,* " frequently and most eminently useful in obtaining by personal communication with the authorities, and even peasants of Sardinia, supplies of fresh provisions, vegetables, fruit, &c. for the fleet, which could not have been procured by any person less conversant with the language and manners of the natives."

Dr. Scott, in speaking of himself, says, that he " was employed in matters of great confidence, and not to be written, in regard to Sardinia, and, in fact, was the organ of communication between Lord Nelson and the Duke de Genevois, brother to the King of Sardinia, and then viceroy. And that other essential services were rendered by him, acting under the direction and instructions of Lord Nelson, so that, by a good understanding and intelligence with the government of that island, unlimited supplies of fresh provisions, &c. were obtained for the fleet, notwithstanding the *strictest edicts*

* Vice-Admiral Sir William Parker, K.C.B.

and proclamations, forbidding them beyond a certain extent—*i. e.* ample supplies were obtained *without committing the neutrality of Sardinia.*"

Thus it was that Dr. Scott's peculiar talents, and natural propensity to seek out wherever he went, the characters and customs of the inhabitants, and still more, his happy art of making friends, became of the utmost use in the emergency in which the fleet was placed; and so generally successful were his efforts in this line, that Lord Nelson lost no opportunity of sending him in the frigates in advance, to prepare supplies at the different ports to which the fleet resorted to replenish.

It must not be supposed that the French authorities could be kept in entire ignorance of what was going on in Sardinia; on the contrary, knowing a something, and suspecting a great deal more, the severest remonstrances poured in upon the viceroy from the French commissary, in one of which he threatens to report to his government so flagrant a breach

of the neutrality—" Le gouvernement de la ré-
publique," writes the Frenchman, " a droit de
se plaindre de cette excessive complaisance !—
nourrir régulièrement une escadre, qui bloque
un port, la ravitailler, en un mot, periodique-
ment, c'est fouler aux pieds la neutralité que
l'on, dit professer, &c.—Je vais faire part à mon
gouvernement d'un fait, qui mérite toute son
attention, et dans lequel, il m'est penible, de
voir quelques motifs de mésintelligence entre
la France et sa majesté Sarde."

   The Sardinian government, having no means
of defence, or resources for engaging in open
hostility with France, complied officially with
the neutral regulations by giving public orders
for limited supplies, but it continued favourable
to the English, and the commandantes of La
Maddalena and Gallura were given to understand at the same time, that it was the wish of
the Viceroy that accommodation of every kind
should be afforded to Lord Nelson's fleet. This
was in November, 1803. On the 11th of

December following, the fleet anchored in the
Gulf of Palmas. Dr. Scott immediately left
the ship to pay complimentary visits from the
admiral in the Islands of St. Pietro and St.
Antioco, the latter of which forms the west side
of the bay, where he was kindly entertained by
the authorities, and each return on board was
accompanied by presents of game, fish, and
other light provisions. After this, the vice-
consuls of the Island were graciously received
in the Victory by Lord Nelson, and, being es-
corted back by Dr. Scott, were again charmed
by his knowledge of their language, and anxiety to become better acquainted with the literature of the Sards, and they reloaded him with
the most acceptable gifts for the admiral's table. The friendly footing thus far established
was soon improved upon. A horse and guide
were provided on another occasion, and a day
spent by the secretary on the coast of Sardinia
in the neighbourhood of Villarios, was followed
by the ships being supplied with water and

provisions for another cruise. This being effected, and after due expressions of kindness on
shore, they weighed anchor, and steered again
to the north. During their long continued
cruise off the north of Sardinia, a pleasing epi-
sode occurred in Dr. Scott's services, in the
acquaintance he formed with a gentleman of
the name of Magnon, a native of Savoy, who, at
the time when they first became known to each
other, was commandant of the round tower of
Longo Sardo, in the district of Gallura, a romantic fort, strongly defended both by nature
and art, which is situated on an eminence at
the natural harbour of Longon, directly facing
Bonifazio, in Corsica. The country about it
is wild in the extreme, and almost desolate,
being only thinly inhabited by shepherds, who
watch their flocks night and day with arms, to
defend them against the incursions of the bar-
barians, who occasionally ravage their coast.
In the fort, his " philosophical retreat," as he
called it—with a small garrison under him,

dwelt Francis Paul Magnon, once a gay soldier, happy and prosperous—now broken in hope, and with a poetical fancy, brooding over the memory of better days. In the previous war, during the government of Robespierre, he had been severely wounded, and suffered tedious imprisonment, and he had sustained, too, the loss of ties and fortune, the remembrance of which, in this uncongenial banishment, ever corroded in his mind, and created the deepest detestation of the French republic. Like Boetius, however, he sought consolation in philosophy and the muses. His "Nuits Maritimes," a series of poems in the French language, on the most solemn subjects, remain records of his religion, loyalty, and sufferings, as well as of his poetical skill. Separated for several years from a widowed mother, whom he tenderly reverenced, and from his wife and child, the objects of his dearest affection, and ascribing all the bitterness of his lot to the agency of the French nation, we may conceive with what delight he

hailed the presence of a power in the Mediterranean able to cope with the enemies of his
peace. The vigils of many weary nights over
the dark and roaring sea in the direction of his
family, and the unwilling submission to fetters
he had no strength to throw off, seemed all
repaid when he saw from his watch-tower the
English fleet pass like a vision through the
Straits of Bonifazio. The fleet arrived at the
anchorage of Mezzo Schifo, off the island of
Maddalena, on the 24th December, 1803, and,
two days afterwards, Monsieur Magnon was introduced to Dr. Scott, and the illustrious hero,
whom, to use his own phrase, he looked upon
as " the guardian angel of Sardinia."   He was
too hearty a friend to the enemies of France,
from which country he had met with nothing
but hard treatment, to disguise his sentiments,
and, on dining the next day on board the Victory, he was presented by Lord Nelson with
the gold medal of the Nile, and by Dr. Scott,
with Cicero's philosophical works, and a pen,

that had been used by Lord Nelson, in compliment to his good wishes and expressions of devotion. Thus commenced their acquaintance
with this interesting character and very useful
friend, for Magnon made no secret of his desire
to serve them in spite of all prescribed neutrality,
and proved it at once by exerting himself to the
utmost to procure information of the movements
of the republican party in Corsica. On the very
day after he was in the Victory, he wrote to
Dr. Scott an account of the state of the garrison at Bonifazio, which he had obtained from
one of his *half-savages,* as he calls the man,
whom he had sent over as a spy. The details
are amusing and characteristic: " A mon retour
dans ma solitude, j'ai reçu une gondole de
Boniface, sur laquelle, est revenu un de mes
demi-sauvages—beaucoup plus adroit, peut-être,
que ne l'ont crû les Français. Il m'a rapporté,
que cette ville n'a pour le moment que quatre
cents hommes de garnison, dont même la
majeure partie est de la nouvelle levée, que

l'on continue rigoureusement, en leur pro-mettant la dépouille de la Sardaigne. Les enfans même de cette ville couraient après ce bon homme pour le ménacer, de venir manger toutes les provisions de sa cabanne, lorsque l'escadre des *traîtres et féroces Anglais* se serait éloignée : ce sont les douces épithètes, que vous attribue le peuple qui modestement se dit le plus poli de la terre ! Cependant, le Brick détaché de votre escadre le matin du 26 courant s'étant approché de Boniface, mon bon Pasteur vit toute la ville en tumulte courir aux armes. Le Commandant, quoique goutteux, se porta à la marine où toute la troupe était sous les armes, avec la mêche près du canon pour faire feu sur votre navire, s'il se fut approché de quelques toises de plus. Lorsqu'il se fut éloigné, la tranquillité se rétablit," &c.

The singular part, however, of this acquaint-ance, so far as Dr. Scott and Monsieur Mag-non were concerned, was the romantic friendship which the latter formed for Scott, and the abstract subjects of correspondence which voluminously passed betwixt them. Magnon began these literary communications, by sending the first five cantos of his " Nights at Sea," already alluded to, which he describes as composed in the intervals of his official duties; and he refers to a violent apostrophe to the usurper of France, which occurs in one of them, in proof that he had none of the *sang froid* of a philosopher, when he approached that subject. The poem threatens Napoleon with the fate of Cæsar, and recommends to him the example of Monk. This was accompanied by a poem in the dialect of Tempio, with a translation into Italian by Magnon himself, and so much and so deservedly was it admired by Dr. Scott, that we make no apology for inserting it.

CANZONE TEMPIERE.

Palchi non torri dì Tempù passatu
Palchi non torri dì Tempu paldutù.

Torra alta volta torra a fatti meù
Tempu impoltanti tempu preziosù
Tempu che vali tantu cante Deù
Par un Cori ben vistu, e viltuosù !
Tempu a distempu caro, arreù
Di stà in tanti affanni agoniusù,
Cant 'utilosu mi saristi statù
Tempu aenditi a tempu cunnusciutu !
Palchi non torri dì Tempu passatu
Palchi non torri dì Tempu paldutu ?

Tempu che in un cuntinuo muimentu
Poni tutta la to stabilitai,
Retrozedi pal me ch' era ditentu
Candu passesti da un Sonnu grai !
Chi la to chietù lu to assentu
Cunsisti in non stà chiettu mai
A ! Sì turrai tempu mal gastatu
Chi be chi t' arìa ripaltutu !
Palchi non torri, &c.

Tempu chi sempri in giusta prupulzioni
Di lu to motu in giru anda la sfera
N'aggi di me ti precù cumpassioni
Ristorrami a prinzipiù di Carrera ;
Di l' anni l' ultima Staxioni
Torrami alta volta in primaera !
L'Esse lu ch 'era a me sarà nicatù
Chi insensibili tant 'anni ò ottenutu ?
Palchi non torri, &c.

L'Albori nudu Senza fiori, e frondi
Vinutu maggiù a chisti frondi, e fiori ;

A campu siccù tandu corrispondi
Un beddù traggiu d' allegri culori.
Supelvu Salta d' invarru li spondi
Riu di Stiú poarù d' umori,
E l'anticù vigori rinoatú
Non sará mai in un homu canutu !
Palchi non torri, &c.

La Salpi veccia chidd' antichi spoddi
Lassa, e si vesti li so primi gali
Da li cinari fritti in chiddi scioddi.
Chidda famosa cedda orientali
Rinasci, e tantu spiritu ricoddi
Ch' agili come prima batti l' ali,
E l' anima imortali arrifolmatu
No vedra più lu so colpo abbattutu !
Palchi non torri, &c.

La notti pal vinè, la dì s' imbruna
Candu lu Soli mori in occidenti
A luci poì torra tutta in una
Candu rinasci allegru in Orienti ;
E la Soredda la candida luna
Da li mancanti torra a li criscenti ;
E un homù cadenti a chistú statú
Non dè torrà da und' è dicadutú
Palchi non torri, &c.

Non timi tempù carù d' implicatti
In falzi inganni, immaginazioni,
In fatti teli di ragni, in chiddi fatti
Cuntrariù a lu bon Sinnù alla raxioni

In chimeri, in dilirj in disbaratti
Muti di la me paldizioni
N' aggi cumpassioni, tempù amatu
D' un cori afflittù cunfusu, e pintutu.
Palchi non torri, &c.

Si cummincia di nouva vij
Di a usà diffarenti acunomia
Nè palticula mancù di la dì
Senza implialla bè passà ci dia
Chi ben previstu fin a lù murì
Pa l' ultimo viaggiù mi sarìa
O alligria, o tre volti biatu
Tempu candù da te foss' attindutu !
Palchi non torri, dì, tempu passatu
Palchi non torri, dì, tempu paldutu.

FINE.

Not a fortnight elapsed before Monsieur
Magnon wrote again, giving a voluminous description of the customs and manners of the
wild inhabitants of his neighbourhood,—of
the feuds which, as is well known, have for
centuries disgraced the history of Sardinia,
involving its inhabitants in constant bloodshed,
—and of the state of religion and of the clergy
in the northern part of the island, with which

he was more particularly acquainted. The
information respecting the habits of the clergy,
corroborated by personal observation in Spain,
Sicily, &c., made a strong impression on Dr.
Scott's mind, and led him to the consideration
of the many practical evils of the Roman
Catholic system. "I should be stoned to
death," writes Magnon, "if I dared to tell
our Sards my opinion of their religious worship; but I cannot deceive a friend in the
avowal which I make to him, that our theological schools are still covered with the dust
of the scholastic cavillings of the middle ages.
They still hold to the subtlety of the ancient
schools, and neglect but too much the instruction of the people in the sublime practical
morality of Jesus Christ. Two great incon-
veniences are the consequence: the one, that
religion has more of the exterior practice of
the Pharisee, than of the interior conviction
and compunction of the Publican. The other
is, that our priests weary themselves in study-

H

ing words; and content with the respect which
a long cassock gives, they think more in
general of living at their ease, than of instructing their flocks. They are satisfied when the
sheep enter the fold at the appointed hour,
but they concern themselves but little in min-
istering to them food and the word, and in
cleansing the *wool* of their consciences. This
species of neglect is only too strongly proved by
facts. Woe to him who shall eat meat on a
Friday—he would be a long time bargaining
for his absolution; but they would make little
noise about the grossest immoralities.

"I will cease, Monsieur le Docteur, to weary
you with a too insipid detail; you must remember
that it is a soldier who writes to you, and upon
a subject so far out of his line, and so much
above his powers. I should soon have all our
clergy upon my hands, if it were known that
I had given a protestant to understand that
divine worship here is rather a tribute of the
lips than a homage of the heart."

Magnon's description of the effect of the feuds presents an appalling picture. The detestable assassinations committed, were computed by him to carry off yearly more than five hundred men, almost always in the flower of their age. " Judge," he writes, " of the influence of prejudice upon the population! You will be astonished, perhaps, that, among these ferocious men the philosophy of vengeance should have its sophisms. Many times, in my intercourse with my Charibs, I have combated revenge by the decalogue, the Lord's prayer, and other parts of the scriptures, and, above all, by the death of our Saviour, after having first asked them whether they were Christians. They answered me that my principle must give way before the law of nature. When enmity is declared, say they, if I do not kill my enemy, I am sure that he will kill me. I am, therefore, in a position of natural defence, and in killing him, I no more sin against the commandments than a soldier who kills an enemy in war. To

kill a person in self defence is not to commit
homicide. When I touched them upon the
motives of religion, and the resource of civil
justice to revenge their wrongs, these good people told me that civil justice only listened to
those who brought gifts; but if I would lay
aside my uniform and preach to them all in
this manner they would very soon abandon a
prejudice which in reality kept them in a per-
petual torture."

Monsieur Magnon, being one day in the
Victory, expressed a wish that some of the
officers and even the Admiral himself would
attend one of the religious festivals of the country, shortly to be held at the small town near
his fort, the sight of which he thought would
gratify them, as their presence would certainly
please the people. Several of the ship's company, being much interested by his representations, promised to be present. Before the
festival took place, however, the fleet left the
Maddalene Islands, and, shortly after, anchored

in the Bay of Rosas, in the north of Spain.
Here the usual communications were held
with the shore, and a number of Spanish newspapers, among other things, were sent to the
Admiral, and were duly read to him by his
foreign secretary. In them a great sale of
pictures, books, curious bibles, church plate,
dresses, &c. was announced, and attracted
Scott's antiquarian taste. Nothing was said
at the time, but it seemed to have dwelt in the
Admiral's mind, for at dinner, talking jocosely
with Dr. Scott, he said to him, " I know why
you dwelt so much upon the advertisements in
the Spanish papers—ah ! my dear doctor, you
are always the same. You want a holiday, I
suppose, and would be glad to have a run on
shore at Barcelona, and ruin yourself in old
Spanish books and curiosities, as you have done
before. You dwelt upon the advertisement to
give me a hint—that's the plain English of the
matter—well," he continued, turning to the
officers, " can we spare Dr. Scott ? you see I

have half a mind to gratify you. Well, we must send into Barcelona for supplies, so I'll try and indulge you." This was all that took place openly on the subject, but Dr. Scott, having received his private instructions, a signal was made for the Juno frigate to come alongside, and the following day, towards evening, she was despatched for Barcelona, with the doctor on board. They anchored off the town, and Scott, slipping quietly on shore, passed an hour at the theatre; and, the next morning, began to execute his commissions.

In the course of a few days he returned to the ship, when a number of large chests were hoisted on deck with him, which excited no small amusement, from the extensive addition which it seemed the doctor had been making to his floating library. What the chests really contained was not known, until the party from the ship attended the festival recommended by Monsieur Magnon, when they discovered that the plate and vestments which decorated the

altar and priests, and, in short, all the most
distinguished ornaments of the spectacle, had
been presents from the Admiral; and that he
had employed his secretary to buy them for
him at the Barcelona sale, for the purpose of
cultivating the good-will of the people of Sardinia. The Sards had acknowledged the compliment by an enthusiastic inscription in the
chapel to the praise of their benefactor; and
the English officers were thus gratified by an
instance of judicious kindness in their chief,
which proved him as skilful in securing friends,
as they had ever found him in subduing enemies. Another curious proof of Lord Nelson's
good-humoured policy may be cited in his per-
mitting the Latin poets of Sardinia, to compliment him with their verses, whilst he joined
with his zealous secretary, to whose taste such
effusions were more congenial, in appreciating
the expressions of admiration and attachment
with which these worthy votaries of the muse

addressed him. Carbonius, who is duly noticed
in Captain Smyth's, R.N., valuable work on
Sardinia, thus writes to his friend Magnon,
" Utinam Nelsoni, ac Schotto, prætereaque ne-
mini, misellulum illud hexastichum exhibuisses!
in istiusmodi latebras non me conjecisses"—
for it seems that some French officer, who had
seen the lines, was offended by them. They
are, however, as follows, and the reference to
the hero's loss of limb is ingenious and the ver-
sification elegant :

> " Ad Nelsonem,
> Franciscus Carbonius,
> Lat. eloq. professor.

> Centimanum, vir summe, Gygen quum trudere cœlo
>   Possis, quis tibi non pareat unimano ?
> Lævam jura mari dantem, Niloque tremendam,
>   Sequana captivis non vereatur aquis ?
> Hæc erit hæc, domitis regum domitoribus, una,
>   Dextera cui sese conferat ipsa Jovis."

We will not trouble the reader with other
specimens of a similar character, but there are
many such of unequal merit.

Other festivals occurred afterwards at Maddalena, to which the spoils of the Barcelona
sale were also made to contribute, in acknowledgment of the kind welcome always given
by the inhabitants, when the fleet resorted to
their excellent harbours. These became a favourite anchorage with the Admiral; and the
sight of the ships passing on their route thither, or seeking the open sea again, often
charmed the lonely philosopher of Longo Sardo
from his studies. He thus rapturously con-
cludes one of his letters to Dr. Scott : " The
sentinel warns me that he sees you in the distance—I fling down my pen to seize eagerly
a miserable pasteboard telescope, which can
only very feebly aid my sight—but my heart
flies far beyond my obscure glass, to present
my most respectful homage to my Lord Duke
Nelson, and to renew to you with ardour sentiments of the most profound respect."

Dr. Scott was sent to Algiers from the fleet,
on an important mission; of which we can un-

fortunately give but scanty particulars. When
Lord Nelson arrived at Gibraltar, in June 1803,
to assume his command, he found there the
English Consul-general of Algiers, who had
been expelled from his post, in the most inde-
cent manner, on account of some suspicion of
the Dey of quite a private nature. This affair,
together with the detention of an English ship
captured by the Algerine cruisers, had become
intricate from the lapse of time, and the Dey's
shuffling explanations by letter. As soon as
Lord Nelson had received instructions from
Government to adjust these differences, he appointed Sir G. R. Keats, who then commanded
the Superbe, to proceed to Algiers for the purpose, and permitted him, at his own particular
request, to take Dr. Scott with him. Captain
Keats made this selection, in consequence of
the high opinion he had frequently heard the
Admiral express of Scott's abilities and honour,
and his knowledge of languages. The dilato-
riness and continued evasion, however, on the

part of the Dey, rendered it necessary that
Captain Keats and his companion should pay
two visits, with a long interval between them,
before a satisfactory reparation could be extorted. Prior to his intercourse with the Algerine authorities on their second expedition, Dr.
Scott took the precaution of translating into
Italian, the instructions by which he was to
act. One of the most delicate points in the
investigation was to discover whether, and how
far the Dey's conduct was influenced by French
politics. Three years before this, an English
fleet had saved Algiers from being attacked
and plundered by Buonaparte, who wished to
possess it. This was still a favourite object with
him, and it seemed very probable that the ob-
stinacy now exhibited—and which, so long as
it lasted, and the maintenance of peace was
doubtful, precluded of course any English consul from being sent to Algiers—might have
secretly originated in the ingenuity of Buonaparte's emissaries. These would naturally wish

to keep every one away likely to enlighten the
Dey and regency as to their master's nefarious
views : Captain Keats' mission, therefore, had
to awaken the Algerines to the fact, without
seeming to menace them, by hinting at the awk-
ward position they would stand in, if deserted by
England and left to the mercy of France. By
this course they succeeded in obtaining the
amplest apology for the insult offered to our
consul, and the restoration of the captured
vessel, cargo and crew.

The fleet was in port in Sardinia, when the
Superbe returned from her second expedition,
but, on account of her having come from a
country infected by the plague, she could not
immediately obtain pratique. This obstruction
occasioned a letter from Lord Nelson, which is
interesting, from the observation upon Dr.
Scott, which it contains.

TO CAPTAIN KEATS.

Victory, January 15th, 1805.

MY DEAR KEATS,—Many thanks for your

telegraph message, and I am sorry that for
form's sake I must consider you, at least for
one day, in quarantine; but, I think, if Dr. Scott
will go with one of your officers to the shore,
and state to the governor and officers of health
that you have been as many days in quarantine
as you have been from Algiers, that the place
is healthy, and you are healthy, with such win-
ning ways as Dr. Scott knows so well how to use,
I have no doubt but that you will have pratique ;
and let your officer say that I have examined
the state of the ship, and find her proper to
have pratique, &c., &c., &c., which I am ready
to certify, if the governor wishes it, then I shall
hope to have you to dinner, but if they will not
give you pratique, I shall to-morrow. Ever,
my dear Keats, your much obliged,

NELSON AND BRONTE.

I send you some late papers.

Besides Dr. Scott's conferences with the Dey,
whom he describes as "*porco grandissimo*," and

Vikel Hadge, the marine minister, whom he
considered a man of talent, he had a great deal
of conversation when last at Algiers with Bacry
and Busnach, the celebrated Jew merchants,
whose claims upon France, afterwards remotely
led to open rupture between the two powers,
and at last to the capture of Algiers. The
recollections which Dr. Scott ever retained of
that city were of the liveliest and most delightful kind. His sensations on entering it, were
as if he had been suddenly set down in the
midst of all the enchantments of the " Arabian
Nights," so exactly were the descriptions there,
verified by what he saw around him. He
looked at the flowing garments and graceful
obeisance of the people, and then on his own
tight coat and pantaloons, and he felt himself,
to use his own expression, " a sneaking dog by
the comparison." His daughters well remember accompanying him only two years before
his death to a cosmorama in London, in which
was a view of Algiers, which excited in him the

most vivid recollections of the past. It was
the sea view, as he must have seen it when approaching it on his missions. There was the
formal town—the waters of the Mediterranean,
blue as the sky above them—and, indeed, the
whole scene was so exactly portrayed, as to
affect him to a degree, to which, with all his
extraordinary recollections, he very seldom gave
way. It was one of those overpowering touches
of feeling from the past, which a person, who
suffered so much in the life of his affections,
as he afterwards did, does not often willingly
incur.

In enumerating Dr. Scott's excursions on
shore, we must not omit to mention his passing
some time in Sicily. Whilst in the neighbourhood of Palermo, he derived much pleasure and
amusement from the hospitality of the Bene-
dictine monks of St. Martino, whose convent,
which is on a magnificent scale, is situated in a
wild and romantic valley, and is kept up in a
style of princely grandeur. From its affording

so luxurious a retirement, many of the monks
are the younger scions of the best families of
Italy, and are men of education and taste.
While Dr. Scott was staying there, he was the
means of saving the lives of some travelling
priests, who had taken shelter in the convent
for the night. His love of reading had caused
him to dip deep into the morning hours among
his books, when the thought suddenly occurred
to him, that the priests had gone to sleep in an
adjoining room, and that he had seen a charcoal brazier burning there during the day.
The idea of their possible danger from suffoca-
tion immediately suggested itself. He got up
and knocked at their door, but receiving no
answer, went in, and found as he had apprehended, the charcoal still burning, and the
priests in a heavy sleep. So deep was their
stupor, that, but for his timely assistance it
must have been fatal, and he used afterwards
to say, his love of old books had at any rate been
of use on that *one* occasion, if even he had
never derived any other advantage from it.

He became extremely popular with the
monks during his stay among them, and they
even endeavoured to detain him as one of their
fraternity; one in particular, a young man of
noble person and insinuating address, urged
him to remain, by holding out every induce-
ment that could flatter him. But he put aside
the proposal, saying, he intended to return to
England to marry, and settle in domestic life.
This excuse only brought a smile of contempt to
the lips of the monk, as he observed, " There
was no occasion for that," and proceeded to
unfold such a system of depravity and hypo-
crisy, as utterly confounded and horrified his
hearer. In Sicily he found, however, a more
congenial acquaintance in the Abbate Giovanni
Meli, for whose beautiful poems in the Sicilian
language he entertained the highest admiration, and he visited him in his retreat near
Palermo.

He afterwards procured many of Meli's best
poems set to music, by different Sicilian com-

posers, together with a collection of the national street music of Palermo, which he employed a musician to transcribe for him. The delicate beauty of these airs is very striking, but they have never yet been arranged for publication.

Dr. Scott was also employed under Lord Nelson's direction, at Naples, as a means of communication with the court and the English minister, Mr. Elliot. The following letter from this gentleman to the Secretary of State at Naples, may be cited as a brilliant specimen of the open abhorrence entertained of Buonaparte by his enemies at this crisis.

TO THE SECRETARY OF STATE AT NAPLES.

Naples, August 24, 1804.

Sir,—I return you with many thanks the French Gazettes of this month, which you have had the kindness to send me.

I have read in the Moniteur of the 1st of August, the article in which I am accused of having advocated at Naples, the assassination of Napoleon Buonaparte. I must assure you, Sir, that the Moniteur does me wrong. I should be sorry to see fall under the poignard of an assassin, the victim, who is worthy, by so many titles, to perish by the sword of justice.

I have the honour to be, &c. &c.

H. ELLIOT.

Dr. Scott is still remembered, by some who knew him there, as connected with their most pleasing recollections of Naples' society. A lady who met him frequently, speaks of him as having been at that time " pale, thin, and tall in person, very romantic and enthusiastic ; and in ecstasies on discovering an edition of Tasso in the Neapolitan dialect." He was also devoted to music ; and delighted. every body in the families where he was introduced, by that singular charm of manner, which no one who ever knew him can fail to recall.

We have now adverted to the principal circumstances of Dr. Scott's employments in the
Mediterranean, in the course of the years 1803
and 1804. During the whole of the period,
the fleet continued cruising about from one
point to another, obtaining by this means as
much variety in their tedious service as was
possible. And to no one did the time pass
less wearily than to Dr. Scott. Wherever he
went on shore he had friends to visit.—Dinner-
parties, dances, parties of pleasure to see the
curiosities of the neighbourhood, interchange
of music, and all the amusements of society, he
frequently enjoyed. With Magnon, of Longo
Sardo, he kept up a constant and interesting
correspondence on literary subjects; and in
every place he found some friend to look after
and procure for him the foreign books he
coveted for his library; chests of which were
sent him occasionally from Barcelona, Cagliari,
&c. &c.

In January, 1805, immediately after his

return from his second visit to Algiers, with
Captain Keats—the fleet being then at the
Maddalene Islands—intelligence was received
of the French having escaped from Toulon,
and Lord Nelson sailed southward in pursuit
of them. On the 4th February, Dr. Scott's
journal records their being within one hundred
leagues of Egypt, and continues as follows :

Feb. 6, 1805. Arrived yesterday in sight of
Africa, (the desert country of Lybia;) find ourselves much to the leeward of Alexandria,
owing to an error in our reckoning. Working
to windward all day.

Feb. 7. Got sight of Alexandria, sent a boat
on shore ; finding they had no account there
of the French, made sail with a fair wind for
Gozo, off Candia. Easily distinguished to-day,
Cleopatra's Needle, and Pompey's Pillar.

Feb. 8. Continued our course with a fair
wind, although it has changed from N.E. to
S.E. This is, I believe, the true *Sirocco*, and
occasions a peculiar sensation ; feel parched.

Feb. 9. Wind fair.

Feb. 10. Wind against us, having suddenly changed at two o'clock in the morning : blows now very heavily indeed from the north. No prayers to-day.

Feb. 11. Phœbe joined. See Mount Ida in Crete, sixteen leagues distance. Left the Victory and came on board the Phœbe—going to Malta.

Feb. 12. Fair wind. Began to read the " Art of Tormenting," a book which I never saw before, and written by Miss Collier.

Feb. 13. Wind strong and unfavourable. Finished the " Art of Tormenting ;" began D'Anquetil's Memoirs.

Feb. 14. Read D'Anquetil's Memoirs— looked at some treatises on the art of Perspective ; a study which appears interesting, and of which I am wholly ignorant.

Feb. 15. Wind not favourable. Finished to-day, D'Anquetil's Memoirs of Louis XIV., &c.

Feb. 16. Wind foul.

Feb. 17. Sunday.   Wind more favourable.
No prayers, not having with me my canonicals.

Feb. 18. Wind fair, arrived this evening at
Malta.   Visited Sir Alexander Ball, General
Villette and Lady B——.

Feb. 19. The fleet off, and bore up with a
fair wind, went on shore.   Dined with Dr.
Thomas, slept at Wilkie's.

Feb. 20. Music at Mrs. Peacock's, dined at
General Villette's, ball in the evening, supper
and singing.

Feb. 21. Took leave of all, and embarked;
Phœbe could not get out.   Hydra came in from
off Toulon.

Feb. 22. Phœbe sailed with convoy.   Foul
wind.

Feb. 23—27. Wind foul.   To leeward of
Malta these two days.   Wind strong at N.W.

Feb. 28. Read since leaving Malta, Junius's
Letters, New Bath Guide, and some of Virgil.
To-day spoke some vessels from Scala Nuova,
a place near Smyrna.

March 1. At sea. Wind contrary.

March 2. Returned to Malta. Dined with Sir Alexander Ball. General Ramsay's in the evening.

March 3. Church, went to St. Antonio, with Sir A. and Lady Ball; dined with Dr. Sewel; and spent the afternoon at Major Peacock's.

March 4. Looked at Mr. Macaulay's books for sale. Dined with General Villette; cards and music in the evening.

March 5. Giorno di partenza. Took leave of the ladies, general, and governor, &c. &c., and left Malta harbour in the evening.

March 6. At sea, wind contrary.

March 7. Do. spoke a ship from Marseilles. Newspapers.

March 8. Do. Regret the death of Lord Proby, and my dear friend Jarvis.

March 9. Wind foul.

March 10. Wind fair,—11, 12, do. do.

March 13. Fine weather, see the land about Cagliari.

March 14. Spoke Termagant; fleet been to Pula and Palmas, and returned to Toulon. Anchored in Palmas in the night.

March 15. Went on shore. Capell ordered off Toulon.

Lord Nelson's return to his old station was occasioned by the news that the French fleet had been dispersed in a gale, and had put back to Toulon. No further entry occurs in the journal, until the 27th of April.

April 27, 1805. Not a word written in my pocket-book for forty-three days! In this time the frigate Ambuscade, Admiral Louis, is come from England. I am come on board my sea house Victory. News of the French fleet, that it sailed away from Toulon on the 31st of last month. We have been to Cagliari and Palermo. Returned back westward, and at last learned that the enemy has passed by Gibraltar. We were detained many days by bad weather and wind. To-day we see the Spanish coast, islands Iviza, Formentera, &c.

April 27. Victory. Read lately Herbert Marsh's History of Politics between Great Britain and France. Finished Robertson's History of Charles V., Letters on Taste, Gorvani's Travels in Italy, play of John Bull, and other comedies, Tears and Sighs of P. P. Gratitude is the memory of the heart.

April 28, second Sunday after Easter. Read the prayers. This morning we have a good wind from the east. We go in sight of the Spanish shore near Alicant.

April 29. We are going with a good wind. We see the Spanish coast. Wrote letters to my friend Capell, also to Wilkie and Magrath.

April 30. Bad wind.

May 1. Bad wind from N.W. A corvette from England. Papers up to the 16th of last month. The head lord of the Admiralty has lost his office.

May 2. Company to dinner. Wind not good.

May 3. Unfavourable wind. Near the shore of Africa.

May 4. Cast anchor in Tetuan Bay. Sent people on shore to fetch water. Decade arrived from Gibraltar.

May 5. Left Tetuan Bay.

May 6. Arrived in the harbour of Gibraltar, but because the wind has just come from the east we have sailed away.

The fleet had been for so long a time baffled by contrary winds in the Mediterranean, that the favourable change just spoken of was quite unexpected by them. So much so, that officers and men had gone on shore, and the linen was landed to be washed. Lord Nelson, however, observing and weatherwise as he was, perceived an indication of a probable change of wind. Off went a gun from the Victory, and up went the Blue Peter, whilst the Admiral paced the deck in a hurry, with anxious steps, and impatient of a moment's delay. The officers said, " Here is one of Nelson's mad pranks." But he was nevertheless right, the wind did become fa- vourable, the linen was left on shore, the fleet cleared the Gut, and away they steered for the West Indies. This course Nelson pursued solely on his own responsibility, there being a variety of opinions as to the route the enemy had taken; some saying, " They had gone to Ireland;" some to this quarter, some to that. " If I fail," said he to Dr. Scott,—" if they are not gone to the West Indies, I shall be blamed: to be burnt in effigy, or Westminster Abbey is my alternative !" Dr. Scott always considered that Nelson never exhibited greater magnanimity, than in his decision on this occasion. The journal proceeds.

May 7, 1805. Good wind.

May 8. Saw Cape St. Mary's: the wind not good.

May 9. The frigate Amphion joins the fleet with the Tiger and transports. At night we came into Lagos Bay.

May 10. All the people on board the transport ship gone to work, and to get provisions.

May 11. At ten o'clock left Lagos Bay.

Sent letters to England by the Wasp. After dinner we met the Queen and Dragon, with transport ships, which were conveying regiments. The same ships, with the Royal Sovereign, are gone to Gibraltar. By the Admiral's desire, I have visited the ambassador from Naples to England, on board the Queen. After this, the ambassador came on board to visit the Admiral.

May 12, fourth Sunday after Easter. Performed the Church service to the people. The fleet steers to the west with a good wind.

May 14. These last days I have been very lazy, for I have read no German.

May 15. Saw the land. Porto Santo. Madeira and the rock Desertas. A good wind.

May 16. To-day we have seen a strange ship. They think it was a French privateer. " Well begun is half done :" according to this proverb half our journey is completed.

May 17. Spoke a Portuguese ship—she gives

us no news.   This ship is going to China, with
priests to convert the people there !

May 18. We are going with a soft wind.
We know not where the French fleet is
gone, so we can only say, " Zeit bringt alles
an Tagen"—Time brings every thing to
light.

May 19. We are most anxious to get to Barbadoes.   I performed the Church service to
the crew.   Fine weather.

May 20. I know not what to write—it is the
old story.

May 21. Nothing new—we must take it as
it comes.

June 2, 1805. On board the Amazon—came
here the 30th of May.   Performed Church
service on board the frigate.

June 4. Arrived at Barbadoes—went on
shore ; but first of all visited Admiral Cochrane
on board the Northumberland.   Visited on
shore Mr. Maxwell, N.C., and Lord Seaforth
with his family.   They see our fleet, and quick

I go back on board the frigate Amazon. Came with the Captain of the Victory.

June 5. Last night we took troops on board, with the General's staff—artillery; because the news has reached us that the French fleet is gone to Trinidad—upon this we left Barbadoes immediately.

We may briefly mention at this point, an instance of the liberality and kindness of Lord Nelson's disposition. Having to take a large land force afloat, he could not bear the distinction which always existed in the allowance between soldiers and sailors; the latter having one pound of meat per diem, while the allowance to the former was only three quarters of a pound. He gave orders, therefore, that so long as under his command, the rations to the two services should be made equal.

We give no further details of Lord Nelson's chase of the French fleet to the West Indies, consisting as it did merely in tracking intelligence of the enemy, from one island to

another, until he drove them back to Europe,
and on the 19th of July cast anchor once more
in the Bay of Gibraltar. Here, after a confinement of nearly two years in the Victory,
Lord Nelson, accompanied by Dr. Scott, went
on shore, where they visited the governor and
Admiral Bickerton, General Drummond and
others. Dr. Scott returned the following day
from the ship to preach; and on the 22nd,
the fleet sailed from Gibraltar to Tetuan Bay,
where they took in water and fresh provisions.
They then steered westward; and on the night
of the 25th repassed the Straits of Gibraltar,
being fired at in the early morning from the
battery of Tarifa, but without effect. A few
days afterwards, on their course home to England, they celebrated in the Admiral's ship for
the seventh and last time, the anniversary of
the battle of the Nile, by the performance of
a play. On the 20th of August, Lord Nelson
landed at Portsmouth, baffled, indeed, of his
main object, but with the satisfaction at least

of having driven a recreant enemy some thou-
sand leagues before him, and saved our West
India possessions from the grasp of Buonaparte.
He proceeded immediately to London, whilst
Scott remained amongst his Hampshire connexions; but before the end of the month the
latter followed his Chief to Merton, and became
a participator in the last happy domestic days,
that Nelson was ever destined to know.

CHAPTER VIII.

Re-appointed to the Victory as private secretary, interpreter,
and chaplain—Merton—Trafalgar—death of Lord Nelson
—Dr. Scott returns with the corpse—funeral.

A VERY short time only had elapsed, when the
hero was summoned by Mr. Pitt to councils
in Downing Street, in consequence of the re-
appearance of the combined fleets at sea.
Several times Dr. Scott attended upon Lord
Nelson in Downing Street. The councils followed in rapid succession. It would seem that
Mr. Pitt had received wrong information, for
he persisted that the enemy were in Port
L'Orient, whilst Lord Nelson maintained they
were at Cadiz, and that they would not long
remain there, as there was a famine in the
town. He recommended that a powerful fleet

should be equipped at once, and, at Mr. Pitt's entreaty, that he would himself go out again, resuming his old command, upon his own terms, with carte blanche as to ships, officers, special appointments, and great latitude as to powers, he consented, promising to "*annihilate* the enemy." At the last council, the very day previous to Lord Nelson's departure for Trafalgar, Dr. Scott waited with Mr. Este, the mutual friend of the Admiral and himself, in a private room, till the council broke up. On quitting the council, Lord Nelson came up to them, ordered Dr. Scott to get ready to join him that night at Merton, and said to Mr. Este, taking leave, "I have just settled your business with Lord Liverpool. I am now going to the Admiralty, and I shall order you a passage on board of Captain Bolton's frigate. You will join me with Bolton in six weeks." Besides Dr. Scott as private secretary and interpreter, with a salary of £100 per annum, Mr. Este was to have been one of six young men, all civilians, with commissions from the Foreign Office, who were to assist in the arduous political negociations which the Admiral anticipated.

Alas! six weeks had hardly elapsed from that day, when all the fine plans and prospects, of these at least, had vanished into air, and Nelson was lost to his country!

Dr. Scott proceeded to Merton that night, and became a witness of those regrets which saddened Nelson's affectionate heart, on bidding (what a gloomy presentiment warned him) would probably be a final adieu to his home, and all he held dearest on earth. Often as his pious resignation to the voice of duty on this occasion has been commemorated, we offer it again from Dr. Scott's own handwriting, as copied from the diary.

Extract from Lord Nelson's Diary, Friday, Sept. 13, 1805.

Friday night, at half-past ten, drove from dear, dear Merton, where I left all which I

hold dear in this world, to go to serve my king
and country. May the great God whom I
adore, enable me to fulfil the expectations of
my country ; and if it is his good pleasure that
I should return, my thanks will never cease
being offered up to the throne of his mercy.
If it is his good Providence to cut short my
days upon earth, I bow with the greatest submission, relying that He will protect those so
dear to me, that I may leave behind. His will
be done. Amen. Amen. Amen.

On the 14th, Dr. Scott resumed his old
quarters in the Victory. Mr. Rose and Mr.
Canning dined the same day on board with the
Admiral, and we give a quotation from a letter
subsequently written by the former, which will
show the unvarying interest Lord Nelson felt
in his chaplain, and how strong his desire was
to secure some good prospects for him—an
instance of thoughtful consideration, which
was doubly kind coming as it did, at a mo-

ment when the greatest anxieties must have
oppressed his own mind, and we may add some
forebodings also. " The day before Lord
Nelson sailed last from St. Helen's, I was on
board the Victory with him for some hours;
in the course of which time he talked much
to me about Mr. Scott, (in the hearing of Mr.
Canning whom I carried with me,) commend-
ing him more warmly than ever, and expressing
the strongest and most lively regard for him ;
and I verily believe he had an earnest anxiety
to mark *that*, in any way that could be useful
or grateful to Mr. Scott."

Of the few brief weeks that occurred between
Lord Nelson's leaving England, and his coming
up with the enemy off the Bay of Cadiz, it is
unnecessary for us to offer any details. Dr.
Scott unfortunately lost the private notes he
kept of this period, and the general account
is sufficiently well known. At daybreak on
Monday the 21st of October, the combined
fleet was descried from the deck of the Victory,

at about ten or eleven miles distant to the south-east, Cape Trafalgar being about seven leagues off in the same direction. This day was the anniversary of a festival in the Nelson family, and the Admiral, in slightly superstitious expectation that his battle would be fought on it, had more than once said to Dr. Scott, "the 21st will be our day." A long heavy swell was setting into the Bay of Cadiz, which, with light, favouring breezes, bore the fleet majestically on its course. The enemy awaited them in a well formed line, which became slightly curved on the wind veering to the southward.* Lord Nelson, with one divi-

* The position of the enemy has been described as forming a crescent, which occasioned the following note by Dr. Scott.

" A mistake—the enemy hove to, but the wind was scant, and their line was not so regularly formed as they could desire; as to the crescent, it was all idea. No such thing existed in the mind of Villeneuve or Gravina.

A. J. SCOTT."

This note is corroborated by his friend, the late Captain W. P. Cumby, R. N., who was lieutenant of the Bellerophon, and succeeded to the command of her when Captain Cooke

sion of the fleet stood for the enemy's van, whilst Admiral Collingwood in the Royal Sovereign steered directly for the centre of their line. At half past eleven, the action commenced, by the enemy firing upon the Royal Sovereign, and twenty minutes afterwards they opened their fire upon the Victory; having discharged at her as she approached, single guns, until they found she was within range of their shot, when they poured in their broad-- sides, maintaining an awful and tremendous fire. Before the Victory returned a shot, she had fifty killed or wounded. At four minutes past noon, she commenced firing from both sides of her deck on the enemy. The Santissima Trinidada of 136 guns, and the Bucentaur being on her larboard, and the Redoubtable

fell early in the engagement. " This imaginary crescent was occasioned by the wind veering to the southward after they had formed their line on the larboard tack, which caused the headmost ships to lie up two or three points higher, and consequently brought the sternmost ships far to windward of those which had time to form in the wake of the leading ships."

on her starboard side. While the Victory was
thus engaged, her second, the Téméraire, fell on
board the Redoubtable on the opposite side,
and on board of her beyond was another French
ship. These four ships were lying so close to
each other, that they formed a solid mass, and
every gun that was fired, told. The carnage
on the deck of the Victory became terrific. Dr.
Scott's duties confined him entirely to the cockpit, which was soon crowded with wounded and
dying men ; and such was the horror that filled
his mind at this scene of suffering, that it
haunted him like a shocking dream for years
afterwards. He never talked of it. Indeed
the only record of a remark on the subject was
one extorted from him by the inquiries of a
friend, soon after his return home. The expression that escaped him at the moment was,
" it was like a butcher's shambles." .

His natural tenderness of feeling, very much
heightened by the shock on his nervous system, quite disqualified him for being a calm

spectator of death and pain, as there exhibited in their most appalling shapes. But he suppressed his aversion as well as he could, and had been for some time engaged in helping and consoling those who were suffering around him, when a fine young lieutenant was brought down desperately wounded. This officer was not aware of the extent of his injury, until the surgeon's examination, but, on discovering it, he tore off with his own hand the ligatures that were being applied, and bled to death. Almost frenzied by the sight of this, Scott hurried wildly to the deck for relief, perfectly regardless of his own safety. He rushed up the companion ladder—now slippery with gore—the scene above was all noise, confusion, and smoke—but he had hardly time to breathe there, when Lord Nelson himself fell, and this event at once sobered his disordered mind. He followed his chief to the cockpit—the scene there has been painfully portrayed by those who have written the life of Nelson; his chaplain's biographer has little to add, but that the confusion of the scene, the pain endured by the hero, and the necessity of alleviating his sufferings by giving lemonade to quench his thirst, and by rubbing his body, of course precluded the reading prayers to him in the regular form, which otherwise would have been done—but often, during the three hours and a half of Nelson's mortal agony, they ejaculated short prayers together, and Nelson frequently said, " Pray for me, Doctor." Every interval, indeed, allowed by the intense pain, and not taken up in the conduct of the action, or in the mention of his private affairs, was thus employed in low and earnest supplications for Divine mercy. The last words which Dr. Scott heard murmured on his lips were, " God and my country," and he passed so quietly out of life, that Scott, who had been occupied ever since he was brought below, in all the offices of the most tender nurse, was still rubbing his stomach when the surgeon perceived that all

was over. We subjoin part of a letter from
Dr. Scott to Mr. Rose, in reply to some inquiries from that gentleman, as to Lord Nelson's
mention of himself on his death bed. It must
be understood that this letter does not pretend
to be a full description of what passed, but it will
confirm accounts already given, and cannot
fail to be highly interesting.

"In answer to your note of the 10th inst.
which, forwarded by way of Chatham, I received
this morning, it is my intention to relate everything Lord Nelson said, in which your name
was any way connected. He lived about three
hours after receiving his wound—was perfectly
sensible the whole time, but compelled to speak
in broken sentences, which pain and suffering
prevented him always from connecting. When
I first saw him, he was apprehensive he should
not live many minutes, and told me so, adding
in a hurried agitated manner, though with
pauses, ' Remember me to Lady Hamilton !—
remember me to Horatia !—remember me to

all my friends. Doctor, remember me to Mr.
Rose ; tell him I have made a will, and left
Lady Hamilton and Horatia to my country.'
He repeated his remembrances to Lady Hamilton and Horatia, and told me to mind what he
said, several times. Gradually he became less
agitated, and at last calm enough to ask ques-
tions about what was going on; this led his
mind to Captain Hardy, for whom he sent and
inquired with great anxiety, exclaiming aloud
he would not believe he was alive, unless he
saw him. He grew agitated at the Captain's
not coming, lamented his being unable to go
on deck, and do what was to be done, and
doubted every assurance given him of the Captain's being safe on the quarter deck. At last
the Captain came, and he instantly grew more
composed, listened to his report about the
state of the fleet, directed him to anchor, and
told him he should die, but observed, he should
live half an hour longer.

" 'I shall die, Hardy,' said the Admiral.

" ' Is your pain great, sir ?'

" ' Yes, but I shall live half an hour yet—
Hardy, kiss me.' The Captain knelt down by
his side and kissed him. Upon the Captain
leaving him to return to the deck, Lord Nelson exclaimed very earnestly more than once,
' Hardy, if I live I'll bring the fleet to an anchor—if I live I'll anchor—if I live I'll anchor,'
—and this was earnestly repeated even when
the Captain was out of hearing. I do not mean
to tell you everything he said. After this interview, the Admiral was perfectly tranquil—looking at me in his accustomed manner when
alluding to any prior discourse. ' I have not
been a great sinner, doctor,' said he. ' Doctor,
I was right—I told you so—*George Rose has
not yet got my letter*—tell him'— he was interrupted here by pain—after an interval he said,
' *Mr. Rose will remember*—don't forget, doctor,
mind what I say.' There were frequent
pauses in his conversation. Our dearly beloved
Admiral otherwise mentioned your name, in-

deed very kindly, and I will tell you his words when I see you, but it was only in the two above instances he desired you should be told.

" I have the honour to be, &c. &c.

" A. J. SCOTT.

" H.M.S. Victory, Dec. 22nd, 1805."

Some remark on the private feelings of Lord Nelson will probably be looked for, in the life of his chaplain. To a question put to Dr. Scott as to Lord Nelson's religious sentiments, his answer was, " He was a thorough clergyman's son—I should think he never went to bed or got up, without kneeling down to say his prayers." Dr. Scott also said of him that he had frequently expressed to him his attachment to the Established Church, in which he had been educated, and he proved the sincerity of this, by the regularity and respect with which he always had divine service performed on board the Victory, whenever the weather permitted. After the service he had generally a few words with the chaplain on the subject of the sermon, either thanking him for its being a good one, or remarking that it was not so well adapted as usual to the crew; the Admiral being always anxious that the discourse should be sufficiently plain for the men, and his chaplain, with the liability of a scholar, being sometimes tempted into a too learned disquisition; more than once, on such occasions, has Lord Nelson taken down a volume of sermons in his own cabin, with the page already marked at some discourse, which he thought well suited to such a congregation, and requested Dr. Scott to preach it on the following Sunday.

With regard to his unfortunate admiration of Lady Hamilton, we may safely say, that neither Dr. Scott, nor his other most intimate friends, believed in its criminality. Lord St. Vincent used to call them " a pair of sentimental fools," and it is a fact that Lady Hamilton never was a mother. Certainly, therefore, she had no connexion with Lord Nelson's adopted daughter, as to whose parentage Dr. Scot never gave any clue, whatever he may have known on the subject. But it has been thought by some, who witnessed Nelson's intimacy with royalty at Naples, and were aware that he had been warned· of even the danger of assassina- tion in consequence of it, that Horatia Nelson might lay claim to a far more illustrious origin than has been supposed. This solution, if a true one, accounts equally as well for the mise- rable state of mind which Lord Nelson's let- ters, written from Naples, betray, and which his biographers have attributed to his infatuated attachment to Lady Hamilton. It may be feared that this misery was the consequence of guilt, but, if so, such uneasiness was the con- scientious compunction of an habitually upright mind.

With a genius that fitted him for the very highest place among men, Lord Nelson's habits and feelings were perfectly simple, and the kindness and sincerity of his heart remained unimpaired by all his extensive intercourse with the world. He enjoyed, what seems often denied to the lot of greatness, the private friendship of many worthy men. By none was he more deeply deplored than by Dr. Scott.

TO REAR-ADMIRAL SCOTT.

October 27, 1805. Victory.

MY DEAR UNCLE,—On the 21st instant, the combined fleets, of thirty-three sail of the line, were completely defeated by our twenty-seven sail of the line. The enemy were extended to leeward, and in as good a line as they could well form, with so little wind as there was. Our fleet, in two divisions, went down, all sail set, steering sails, &c. the wind right aft, and the swell forcing the ships down. Lord Nelson in the Victory, led one division, Admiral Colling-wood the other. The first cut through between the enemy's ninth and tenth ship ; the latter, between the nineteenth and twentieth. Never was so complete a defeat. There has been a heavy gale of wind ever since the night of the action, the wind dead on a lee-shore, and we have been lying a wreck part of the time, consequently we know nothing of particular damages, or all the enemy's ships which have been taken. I believe there were, at least, nineteen taken, two three-deckers, one called a four-decker, the largest ship ever built. The Spanish Admiral Gravina, the French Admiral Villeneuve, &c. &c. My dear Uncle, having told you the news, which will make you rejoice for your country; what will you think of me who detest this victory? It has deprived me of my beloved and adored friend—I knew not until his loss, how much I loved him! He died as the battle finished, and his last effort to speak, was made at the moment of joy for victory. I cannot talk more to you about it, I hope soon to see you. I shall attend my dear Lord's remains, and act when I reach England as his executors may direct; let me find a letter from you at Portsmouth, this ship *must go*

home, the mizenmast gone, the main and fore-
masts cut to pieces, and only standing by mi-
racle, &c. &c.   It still blows hard, but we are
in tow by the Neptune, and hope to get the
gut open to-morrow morning.   Possibly, we
shall rig a good jurymast at Gibraltar, and
then go home.   I do not say much of my loss
—it is beyond all utterance—I, of course, now
retire.   With love to my aunt, and Mary, and
with respect,

I am, &c.

A. J. SCOTT.*

---

* " Copy of the log of His Majesty's Ship Victory, October
21, 1805.

   " At four, wore ship ; at six, observed the enemy bearing
E. by S., distance ten or eleven miles, bore up to the eastward ;
out all reefs of the topsails, set steering sails and royals,
cleared for quarters ; at eight, light breezes and cloudy ; body
of the enemy's fleet E. by S., distance nine or ten miles. Still
standing for the enemy's van ; the Royal Sovereign and her
line of battle, steering for the centre of the enemy's line ; the
enemy's line extending about N.N.E. and S.S.W. ; and 11 40″
the Royal Sovereign commenced firing on the enemy, they
having begun firing at her at 11 30″ ; at 11 50″ the enemy

Dr. Scott returned with the corpse to England, and sat up with it every night for more
than a week, whilst it lay in state at Greenwich, and so emaciated and afflicted was his
appearance at the funeral, that many persons,

begun firing upon us; at 12 4″ opened our larboard guns at
the enemy's van.

" Light airs and cloudy, standing towards the enemy's van
with all sails set, at four minutes past twelve, opened our fire
on the enemy's van in passing down their line; at 12 20″, in
attempting to pass through their line, fell on board the tenth
and eleventh ships, when the action became general. About
1 15,″ the Right Hon. Lord Viscount Nelson, and Commander-
in-chief, was wounded in the shoulder; at 1 30″, the Redoubtable having struck her colours, we ceased firing our starboard
guns, but continued engaged with the Santissima Trinidada,
and some of the enemy's ships on the larboard side; observed
the Téméraire between the Redoubtable and another French
ship of the line, both of which had struck. The action continued general until 3 o'clock, when several of the enemy's
ships around us had struck. Observed the Royal Sovereign,
with the loss of her main and mizen masts, and several of the
enemy's ships around her dismasted, at 3 30.″ Saw four sail
of the enemy's van tack, and stand along our line to windward,
fired our larboard guns at those they would reach. At 3 40″
made the signal for our ships to keep their wind, and engage
the enemy's van coming along our weather line. At 4 15″
the Spanish Rear-admiral to windward, struck to some of our
ships which had tacked after them; observed one of the enemy's
ships blow up, fourteen sail of the enemy's ships standing to-

who saw him there, said, "he looked like the chief mourner."

He was distinguished in Lord Nelson's will, by a legacy of £200 bequeathed to "my friend the Reverend Alexander Scott;" and he

wards Cadiz, and three sail of the enemy's ships standing to the southward. Partial firing continued until 4 30", when a victory having been reported to the Right. Hon. Lord Viscount Nelson, K.B. and Commander-in-chief, he died of his wound. At five, the mizenmast fell about ten feet above the poop, the lower masts, yards, and bowsprit all crippled; rigging and sails very much cut, the ships around us much crippled; several of our ships pursuing the enemy to leeward. Saw Vice-Admiral Collingwood's flag flying on board H.M.S. Euryalus, and some of our ships taking possession of the prizes. Struck topgallantmasts, got up runners and tackles to secure the lower masts. Employed clearing the wrecks of the yards and rigging, wore ship, and sounded in thirty-two fathoms, sandy bottom. Stood to the southward under the remnants of the foresail and main topsail, sounded from nineteen to thirteen fathoms. At two, wore ship; at day-light, saw our fleet and prizes, forty-three sail in sight still closing with our fleet. At six, Cape Trafalgar bore S.E. by E., distance four or five leagues. At 6 30" saw three of the enemy's ships to leeward, standing towards Cadiz. Fresh breezes and cloudy, employed knotting the fore and main rigging, and fishing and securing the lower masts. Struck the foretopmast for a fish for the foremast, which was very badly wounded; at noon fresh breezes and hazy."

had a mourning ring given him, which in
design is a very beautiful and appropriate
memento. It is a plain thick gold hoop, with
the duke and viscount's coronets in coloured
enamel, and is simply inscribed within, " Lost
to his country, Oct. 21, 1805." We would
here observe, with due submission to Dr. Scott's
late friend Sir W. Beatty's report of the examination of the body six weeks after death,
that whatever appearances may then have been,
it was considered by those about Lord Nelson,
that his constitution was altogether worn out.
He was subject to frequent pain in the side,
occasioned by the stroke of a spent ball, which
a medical gentleman, intimate with him,
thought, had produced chronic disease of the
liver; he would also express himself, as conscious of the sense of a shattered frame, and,
as looking anxiously forward to repose. The
sight of his remaining eye was fast failing. Had
he survived Trafalgar, he would have liked the
office of Lord High Admiral, and to have had

the entire management of the service; and,
there is no doubt, he would have taken an active
part in politics, for which he was eminently
qualified.

The portrait of Lord Nelson, prefixed to this
work, is engraved from a very beautiful miniature sketch from life, by Jackson.

The drawing came from the possession of Sir
Thomas Lawrence, into the hands of a gentleman, who has kindly allowed an engraving to
be made from it, which is now published for
the first time.   When Dr. Scott saw the sketch,
he put his hand before his eyes, so foicibly
did it recall the countenance of his lamented
patron.

CHAPTER IX.

Is made D.D. by Royal mandate—disappointed about the stall at Canterbury—letters from Lady Hamilton—Sir Thomas Hardy, &c.—Mr. Rose—Mr. Canning—Colonel Bosville—Lady Hamilton.

WE come now to a period in Dr. Scott's life, of far different scenes and feelings than what had hitherto employed it. After the interment of his patron and friend, his connexion with the navy ceased, and the one object he had in view was to obtain a reward in his profession, for services which had been so highly valued by the greatest admirals of the day, and in the course of which his health had so materially suffered. He had a reasonable hope, as will appear, of a prebendal stall at Canterbury, but as a preliminary step to preferment, he

K 3

wished to take the Doctor in Divinity's degree.
His name, however, being off the boards of the
university, it was necessary for him to reside
a term at Cambridge, in order to become a
member again, and be capable of graduating
as D.D.   During this residence, the heads of
colleges and other leading men showed him
the greatest attention ; and were surprised,
considering his active public life on naval
service, at his extensive scholastic acquirements
and theological erudition.   Under ordinary
circumstances, twelve years must elapse betwixt the M.A. and D.D. degrees, during which
period, the name of the party must remain on
the college books ; but in Scott's case, in
compliment to Lord Nelson's memory, and in
acknowledgment of his own merit, the university thought fit to grant him the D.D. degree
by royal mandate,—a highly flattering distinction, inasmuch as the Sovereign's mandate is
made to supersede the statutes of the university, and is never granted but upon the petition

of the university itself. The Prebend at
Canterbury, to which he was looking forward,
was held by the brother of the departed hero,
who being created an earl, with the prospect
of £10,000 a-year, it was everywhere expected
would resign the stall. Dr. Scott's pretensions
to it, in the event of his vacating, were founded
upon the late Lord Nelson's frequently expressed wishes to that effect. Of his plan for
accomplishing the transfer, the hero had spoken
openly the very day they sailed on the last
fatal expedition. "Only you remain quiet,"
he said, "let me get my brother a step, that
is all, and you shall have his. I must not ask
for both now, for the stall is a good thing to
give up to get the deanery; but if I meet the
French fleet I'll ask for both, and have them
too."

This plan Lord Nelson had also mentioned
to Sir Thomas Hardy, who wrote to Dr. Scott,
saying that "every step possible was adopted
by his friends, to secure for him the stall at

Canterbury, but the Earl remained immove-
able;" and it was evidently present to Mr.
Rose's mind, from the following extract from
his letter, dated December 8th, 1805. " I
have reason to believe it will be proposed to
Parliament, to make a grant of a large sum· to
purchase a property to be settled inalienably
on the title of Nelson : if that should take
place, and the Earl in consequence thereof
should relinquish the Prebend of Canterbury,
I have hardly a doubt but that Mr. Pitt would
give it to you."

The Earl was urged to resign by the Prince
himself, by Lord Moira, and by others whom
it seemed hardly possible that he could refuse;
nor did he positively do so, as long as the grant
of £200,000 remained unsettled; though he
argued to Dr. Scott that his brother meant
he should give up the stall *only* on getting the
deanery—that the earldom in short was no
step. A report of what had been the late Lord
Nelson's wishes speedily circulated,—those

wishes having been well known to so many officers in the fleet, and a strong feeling of disapprobation arose against the Earl. Squibs on the subject appeared in the daily papers, and at length Mr. Fuller, M.P. for Sussex, took it up in the House of Commons.

On a bill being brought forward for making a further provision for the family of Lord Nelson, he observed that "the country had by its liberality to the family of the deceased hero, evinced the respect and gratitude which were justly due to his memory. He trusted, therefore, that neither the magnanimity of that illustrious man, nor the generosity of the empire, would be forgotten by those who were to receive profits and honours, on account of the service which the immortal Nelson had performed. He would not then particularise any thing, though his object must occur to many members in the house. He hoped the representative of that family would also show some degree of generosity, and comply with the wish expressed by the illustrious founder of the family in his last moments."

The next day Mr. Fuller received an anonymous letter, falsifying Dr. Scott's pretensions, and accusing him of being the author of the paragraphs in the newspapers, which had ani-, madverted on the Earl's conduct. Mr. Fuller showed this production to Dr. Scott, with whom he was personally acquainted, upon which the latter wrote as follows :

TO EARL NELSON.

Great Portland Street, May 26, 1806.

My Lord,—I beg leave to assure your lordship that I have not, either directly or indirectly, written, or caused to be written, any paragraphs in the newspapers, neither have I been privy to, or countenanced them. I should not have thought it necessary to make such a declaration to your lordship, but for an anonymous letter addressed to Mr. Fuller, M.P. for Sussex, in which I am accused as the author

of them.   As to any promise from my dear
Lord that you should resign your Prebend in
my favour—could I have submitted myself to
the indignity of asserting such a falsehood, I
could hardly have been guilty of the folly of it.

What I have said to my friends is what I
have said to your lordship, when I have solicited your resignation of the stall—" that your
brother's intentions were, if he could advance
you a step higher in the Church, for me to
succeed you in the stall.   That he avowed such
his wishes and intentions, and expressed his
doubts of being able to accomplish both, adding, however, if he met the French fleet and
gained another victory, that it should certainly
be so."   Such were poor Lord Nelson's words;
all promise to me from his lordship was merely
that of exerting himself in my favour, as soon
as you, my lord, should be better provided for.
On these grounds alone I have solicited, and
still most respectfully solicit your lordship's
resignation in my favour.   On these grounds

alone I have stated to friends my claim and
pretensions.

I have the honour to be, &c. &c.,

A. J. Scott.

The Rev. Earl's answer was contained in
about three lines, stating that he was glad to
find Dr. Scott was not concerned in the paragraphs which were daily appearing in the
public prints. Of the rest of the letter he
took no notice whatever.

No impression could be made on the noble
prebendary. The stall was too good a thing
to give up, so this anxious matter, having hung
in doubt for more than a year, distracting
Scott's peace of mind, and injuring his health,
at last ended in utter disappointment.

The following letter from Lady Hamilton, a
fellow sufferer from the blight which passed over
the prospects of many connected with the departed hero, seems highly characteristic of the
writer.

September 7th, 1806.

My DEAR FRIEND,—I did not get your letter
till the other day, for I have been with Mrs.
Bolton to visit an old respectable aunt of my
dear Nelson's. I shall be in town, that is, at
Merton, the end of the week, and I hope you
will come there on Saturday, and pass Sunday
with me. I want much to see you ; consult
with you about my affairs. How hard it is,
how cruel their treatment to me and Horatia.
That angel's last wishes all neglected, not to
speak of the fraud that was acted to keep back
the codicil : but enough ! when we meet we
will speak about it. God bless you for all your
attentions and love you showed to our virtuous
Nelson and his dear remains, but it seems
those that truly loved him are to be victims
to hatred, jealousy, and spite. However, we
have innocency on our sides, and we have,
and had, what they that persecute us never

had, that was *his* unbounded love and esteem, his
confidence and affection. I know well how he
valued you, and what he would have done for you,
had he lived. You know the great and virtuous
affection he had for me, the love he bore my
husband, and if I had any influence over him,
I used it for the good of my country. Did I
ever keep him at home? Did I not share in
his glory? Even this last fatal victory, it was
I bid him go forth. Did he not pat me on the
back, call me brave Emma, and said, " If there
were more Emmas, there would be more
Nelsons." Does he not in his last moments do
me justice, and request at the moment of his
glorious death, that the king and nation will
do me justice? And I have got all his letters,
and near eight hundred of the Queen of Naples's
letters to show what I did for my king and
country, and prettily I am rewarded. *Psha*—
I am above them, I despise them—for, thank
God, I feel that having lived with honour and
glory, glory they cannot take from me. I de-

spise them—my soul is above them, and I can
yet make some of them tremble, by showing
them how he despised them; for in his letters
to me he thought aloud. Look at ———,
courting the man he despised, and neglecting
now, those whose feet he used to lick. Dirty,
vile groveller! But enough till we meet. Mrs.
Bolton and all the family beg their compli-
ments. Write to me at Merton, and ever
believe me, my dear sir, your affectionate,

EMMA HAMILTON.

Horatia is charming. She begs her love
to you. She improves daily. she sends you
100,000,000 kisses.

Even congratulations on success were added
to Scott's mortification on the loss of the stall.
His good friend Magnon wrote *with Lord Nelson's pen,* to compliment him on the attainment
of a bishopric, as he called it; and Sir Thomas
Hardy sent him a warm letter of rejoicing,
having read in the papers that he had obtained
his wishes.

TO THE REV. DR. SCOTT.

Triumph, Lynhaven Bay, Chesapeak,
March 10, 1807.

MY DEAR SCOTT,—I congratulate you, my
good fellow, most sincerely, on your having
succeeded to the stall at Canterbury, and I
hope the Earl resigned with a good grace. - I
see by your letter, that you are hurt that the
newspapers should have taken it up, but I
hope you have too good an opinion of me, to
suppose for a moment that I should think you
gave them the least clue.   No, my dear doctor,
I am certain you never did.   I am quite happy
to hear that Beatty is appointed to the Channel
fleet.   I still hope that all that served under
our ever-to-be-lamented friend and patron will
be provided for.   God knows the loss both to
you and myself, has been great indeed; I every
day feel it more and more, and never felt his
real loss till now.   Do, my dear doctor, write
to me, and tell me all the news.   I wrote to
the Earl, and sent him a pipe of Madeira, I have

not heard from him. Do tell me if he has
received it. I have also written two or three
times to Lady Hamilton, but have had no answer. In fact it appears that all my friends
have forgotten me, since the loss of my real
friend; and I feel the service so totally different
to what I have been accustomed to, that I
have almost a new profession to learn. When
you see Lady Hamilton, do give my very best
respects to her. I believe she thinks me in-
sincere. I am sure you know to the contrary,
and I wish I knew how to prove to her Ladyship
how much I esteem her for the sake of him who
is no more, and I am sure I shall never forget his
last words to me, "Do be kind to poor Lady
Hamilton." We are blocking two French line
of battle ships and a frigate, and I expect to
be here all the summer. Therefore do write.
Wishing you every happiness,

I remain, My dear Scott,

Your very sincere friend,

T. M. HARDY.

Scott had also to undergo soon after, sus-
pense almost as harassing, with regard to the
living of Cold Norton, which terminated equally
unfortunately, and in addition to these trials,
together with the refusal of the Admiralty to
recognise in any way his diplomatic services,
as being out of the line of his profession, he
found his pay stopped for the periods he had
been absent from his ships upon those very
services which had gained him so much distinction and honour with his admirals. He
petitioned against this severity, pointing out the
serious and irrecoverable ill health which had
been the consequence to himself of these employments; that he had lost also his chance of
prize money whilst thus unavoidably absent
from his ships, and that these absences being
reckoned up, had deprived him of so many
months of service that he was left on the three-
shilling list of chaplains of the navy instead of
the four. The petition was rejected by one
board of admiralty, but it was granted by a
subsequent one, through the interest of Mr.

George Rose; not, however, till February, 1808. Mr. Rose then wrote as follows.

TO THE REV. DR. SCOTT.

DEAR SIR,—I have great satisfaction in being able to tell you, that I have succeeded completely in your application; you will now have your pay that was stopped, and your seniority, which increases your half pay.

This gratification is the higher to me, as at the same time that I have procured an *act of justice* to be done to a person for whom I have a personal regard, I feel warmly that I have done what would have been pleasing to a man, if he had been living, for whose memory I shall retain the most affectionate attachment while I continue to exist.

I am, &c., &c.,

GEORGE ROSE.

Old Palace Yard, February 8th, 1808.

Such were the troubles which harassed Scott on his return from sea. He went down to Southminster, but was forced to return. His

health could not bear either the duties or the
climate of the parish, so he lived on in town,
hoping day after day that something would
turn up, and making every exertion amongst
many powerful friends, to whom his claims
were highly interesting. The friends of the
departed hero were anxious to testify their regard for his memory, by doing the best honour
they could, to one who had so ably, faithfully,
and zealously served him, and who had possessed his peculiar esteem and regard.   Among
these Mr Rose, who considered that every one
who belonged to Lord Nelson was a legacy to
himself, was most zealous and devoted, and did
everything in his power to fix the attention of
Government upon Dr. Scott, as a man closely
connected with Lord Nelson's memory, who
enjoyed his friendship and confidence in an
eminent degree, and who, as such, ought to
share in some degree, in the posthumous re-
compense due to the fallen hero.

But none were more warm, or took more
trouble in the cause, than the Countess of

Liverpool, and her sister, Lady Elizabeth Foster, whom Dr. Scott knew independently of his patron, and who honoured him by their continued private friendship through the years of his retirement in married life. His oldest and much attached friend, Lady Lavington,* also spoke to the Prince and others in his behalf. Every possible quarter was canvassed for him, from the crown down to private patronage. Every body wished to serve him, for everybody liked him, independently of his public merits.

At the end of two years, one of those who had most warmly advocated Dr. Scott's cause, declared that he could only confess he most deeply lamented that he had not with his utmost and strenuous exertions been able to do good to any one person for whom his late invaluable friend (Lord Nelson) was interested. In asking Mr. Canning to lay his case before the Duke of Portland, Scott at last speaks

* The wife of Sir Ralph Payne, created Lord Lavington, see page 3.

even with bitterness : " I solicit your forgiveness, but something stronger than motives of
interest forces me to trouble you with my claim,
for I cannot be neglected, without being at the
same time disgraced."

We close these details of his unsuccessful
efforts for preferment, by the remarks of a con-
temporary and friend, whose authority and experience in public life make them valuable.
" Scott," says he,* " undoubtedly did not receive at the hands of the governments which
ruled the nation in succession, that consideration which was most justly his due.   Not that
he had drawn down upon himself any enmity,
he was too clever and too kind-hearted to provoke it.   I apprehend his case to have been one
lamentably common ; his great patron was no
more, and not only was thus his most powerful

---

* We are permitted to give the name of the Right Hon.
Sir George Rose, who, in concluding these remarks, ex-
presses his delight in " throwing one flower at least on the
grave of his talented, accomplished, and excellent friend."

support snatched from him, but the selfishness of man appreciated less and less, day by day, the services of him who had no more to render, and felt less and less the desire, and even the duty of honouring or rewarding those, who, by contributing to the success of his plans and enterprises, had obtained his esteem, affection, and confidence."

Before withdrawing Dr. Scott altogether from the life of alternate hope and mortification, which his late exertions led to, we would remind the reader that perhaps not the least of his trials at this period, was the tantalizing recurrence of justifiable expectation, which his intercourse with some of the highest society in London naturally occasioned. What must have been his hopes in the atmosphere of Devonshire house, or under the patronage of Lord Moira, or when enjoying the friendship and kind hospitality of Lord and Lady Liverpool, knowing at the same time, too, that the Prince and the Duke of Clarence had both condescended

to interest themselves in his cause ?   In spite,
however, of all this, and the endeavours made
to procure the stall for him, one effort was
wanting, which, certainly he could hardly expect would be made, and as certainly no one
could have expected would be required.   Scott
saw clearly throughout that the only way to
secure the stall, would be that the Lords of the
Treasury should point out to the Earl that what
government was about to do for him, in raising
him to the peerage, with a grant of £200,000,
in memory of his brother's services, *necessarily
involved the resignation of his stall at Canterbury.*
This stipulation, however, was too much to
look for, and Scott stood, as he expressed it,
" like the hare with many friends."

A little incident that took place on one occasion at Fife House might serve to correct an error,
which has become very general, in pronouncing
the name of Nelson's last great victory. Dr. Scott
was one day dining there in company with Mr.
Canning, when the latter very mysteriously let

him into the *secret* (which he as cautiously di-
vulged to the rest of the company before the
evening was over) that a poem by himself was
to be published the next day, in which the
grand naval triumph would be celebrated. He
repeated some of the lines for Scott's opinion,
who immediately found fault with the accent
being thrown on the middle syllable, instead
of on the last in the word Trafalgàr. Mr. Canning defended his pronunciation by the example
of Gibráltar. Such a discussion as this led to
Scott loved to his heart, and gave his opponent
the pronunciation of Gib-ral-tàr* with the most
delicate precision, informing him that it was
only an English corruption which miscalled
that word as it is generally spoken.

Dr. Scott first became acquainted with Mr.
Canning at Colonel Bosville's, a gentleman of
fortune, who spent the winter months at his
house in Welbeck-street, where, punctually at

---

* Gibraltar is a corruption of Gibel Tarik, the mountain of
Tarik, a Moorish General, who first led the Moors into Spain,
A.D. 710.—*Butler.*

five o'clock every day (if we remember rightly) a plain dinner was prepared for about a dozen persons. The guests consisted of some of the most distinguished men of talent of the day, who had the entrée of the house, and a general invitation to dine there whenever it was agreeable to them, provided they were never later than the appointed hour. This society included Mr. Canning, Sir Francis Burdett, Horne Tooke, Curran, and other remarkable political and literary characters. Dr. Scott was introduced amongst them, and, during the year 1806, frequently attended their delightful meetings.

It may be supposed, that, after Scott's return from sea, he had little wish, as he had little opportunity, for renewing his associations with Lady Hamilton. He had known her well during his intimacy with his lamented patron, and had been the frequent witness of her peculiar fascinations. She had an heroic spirit great personal attractions, and much cleverness, and at Merton, in Clarges-street, and in Picca-

dilly, where Scott was frequently summoned to
participate in the festivities, or to assist on important occasions of business, he had admired
her many accomplishments, and been amused
by her dramatic personation of different characters. Though the country did nothing for
her, she was left, at Lord Nelson's death with
means sufficient to fulfil his wishes in the education of Horatia, having at least £1,400 a year,
beside the little estate at Merton, but her
vanity and extravagance found this no compe-
tency. A friend of the Merton coterie was one
day hailed from a carriage window in London
by the voice of a lady, whom he recognised as
Lady Hamilton, and who immediately requested
him to return home with her to dinner. He
pleaded an engagement, but was obliged to
promise to visit Merton the following day.
He had no expectation of meeting any company, and was, therefore, not a little astonished
on his arrival to find what guests were assembled. Signor Rovedino and Madame Bianchi,
with other birds of the same feather, were

regaled by her ladyship on this occasion, with
a sumptuous dinner; and, after the ladies
retired, the superb wines of the Merton cellars,
gifts of crowned heads, &c., were liberally
dispensed by Rovedino, as master of the cere-
monies. The friend we have alluded to was
in the garden next morning, long before the
breakfast hour, and was at length joined there
by Lady Hamilton, with whom he ventured to
remonstrate on the mode of life she was pursuing, and the company she had treated him
with. She attempted to justify herself by saying, that, " it was a less expensive plan than
taking Horatia to town for singing and Italian
lessons." Her friend, however, would not
admit her excuse, and, at length, extorted the
sorrowful confession, that her affairs were
already in a state of grievous embarrassment.
He talked seriously and sincerely with her,
and agreed to find the means of relieving her.
In a few days they had another interview, when
he introduced a gentleman, who had retired
from commercial engagements, but was well

skilled in all matters of finance, and who undertook, on Lady Hamilton's promising to comply
with his conditions, to investigate the whole
state of her affairs, and remedy them, if it
were possible. On looking into them, he found
that two or three years' retirement in Wales
upon a small annuity, would suffice to release
her from all her difficulties. Into Wales she
accordingly went, but it was only for a short
season;—the harp and the viol were soon re-
sounding from her lighted apartments in Bond-
street, wilder extravagances than ever were
committed, and she was again a suppliant for
relief to the friends whose advice she had dis-
regarded. The financier was again appealed
to; but this time he refused his aid, avowing
openly, that all attempts to save a person of
her character must be in vain. Distress soon
after pursued her abroad : and it is well known
that she died in great poverty, having gone
through one of the most extraordinary careers
that ever fell to the lot of her sex.

CHAPTER X.

Marries—resides at Burnham—his children—manner of life—
   death of Mrs. Scott—exertions in his parish—is presented
   to Catterick—made King's chaplain.

PREVIOUS to Dr. Scott's joining Lord Nelson
in the Victory, in 1803, he had renewed his
acquaintance with the family of Mr. Ryder, of
the Charter-house.   We say renewed—because
they had been kind to him when a schoolboy
at the Charter-house, more than twenty years
before.   Mary Frances Ryder was the eldest
daughter, and was just turned seventeen when
Scott was re-introduced at her father's house.
She was then in person tall and well-formed,
with dark blue eyes, and a profusion of auburn
hair, and her letters show that she must have
possessed a resolute mind and clear under-

standing, with a feeling heart. Though Scott
was twice her age at this time, there is no
doubt she was struck and interested by his
romantic spirit, with which her own perfectly
accorded; and being quite equal to appreciating intellectual superiority, she admired it
as displayed in him, to an extent which she
had never met with before. However transient
their first impression of each other might have
proved had they never met again, certain it
is that such an impression was received on both
sides, and that it considerably enhanced the
pleasure of their subsequent intercourse.

That she had taken great interest in his fate
during those eventful years which closed the
war, is very evident, for when the name of
" Scott "* was reported in the list of killed on

* This was John Scott, Esq., public secretary to the Commander-in-chief. He was almost torn in two by a shot from
the enemy, before the action fairly commenced. After death
from a gun-shot wound, the countenance generally remains
placid; but it was not so in this case. Mr. Scott fell very
near to where Lord Nelson was talking with his captain;

board the Victory at Trafalgar, creating of
course the utmost apprehensions amongst Dr.
Scott's friends, Miss Ryder (with her mother)
was amongst the first at the Admiralty, to
inquire after his safety.

His feeling for her was most faithfully retained. He had spoken of it to Lord Nelson,
who, in return, encouraged him with the
highest hopes in his profession, and made him
promise to name his first child after himself.
Alas! there is nothing so melancholy as the
review of that particular season in the life of
the departed, which was consecrated by love!
If this be true as a general remark, it applies
with double force to the case in question; for
no two people ever came together more capable
of enjoying domestic happiness, or who sacri-
ficed more in feeling to obtain it, or who built

Nelson asked him who that was? and, (as Sir T. Hardy
related the story,) on being told, exclaimed, " Poor Scott!
how little I thought that he would be the first to quit this
world ! "

more hopes upon it; and few, perhaps, were ever visited with more interrupting afflictions.

When Dr. Scott returned from the war, he was received in Mr. Ryder's family with the greatest cordiality. He naturally excited that interest there, which the intimate friend and companion of Lord Nelson met with on every side, and to the full extent that acquaintance could go, no one could be more acceptable.

He was a frequent visitor at the house throughout the year 1806, and presenting himself under circumstances, which, as we have remarked, were so generally in his favour, it may easily be imagined that a woman thrown much into his society, could not long remain insensible to the preference he decidedly showed for her. She had been a spectator through his means of the part he took in the public funeral of the hero; she heard from his own lips of scenes and persons, which even at this distance of time it is affecting to record; if he was broken in health and constitution, it

was in the service of his country he had suffered; if he was much older than herself, this
inequality was soon lost sight of in a manner,
which, even when he became an old man, retained all its chivalrous homage to the sex.
Moreover, Miss Ryder was in her way a linguist, and she was a good musician; she had,
therefore, books lent her—hints given her in
her studies—songs written out for her, and in
short, she experienced all those marks of interest which are as attractive and powerful, as
the most open declarations of feeling.   Perhaps
a more agreeable addition to a private family
circle, or a man more likely to win the favour
of a woman of sentiment, cannot be imagined,
than Dr. Scott was at the period referred to.
But counter considerations arose, when he
offered himself as a suitor for Miss Ryder's
hand—and his ill health, the disparity of age,
and his still unsettled prospects, were sufficient
objections in the eyes of prudent parents.
Other objections also were raised, and Miss

Ryder was prevailed on by parental authority
to reject Scott's offer, but in so doing she never
pretended to give up her attachment to him.
Her refusal was enclosed by her mother, to
whom he wrote back in all the agony of disappointment, " that his attachment had been
such, it could ill brook the very suspicion of
alloy. She gives me her friendship," he adds,
" gilding her renunciation with some happy
terms of flattering retrospect, which add to the
bitterness of it. She writes to me quite *en
diplomate.* I have in my time known something of that science ; but in that passion of
human nature, with which I have lately for the
first time been intimately acquainted, I detest
diplomacy. I am unequal to it."

    Dr. Scott's accusation of diplomacy in Miss
Ryder, was itself an unconscious act of the
same kind ; for no woman was likely to remain
at rest under such an imputation, when her
own feelings were avowedly engaged. A correspondence was therefore soon connecting them

again, in which Scott combated the objections
against himself, with all the energy of truth
and affection. " Believe not," he writes, "that
I am unworthy or degraded by having *l'usage
du monde*. It is true, with instructions from
Lord Nelson, and particular directions, I have
succeeded upon confidential business in which
I have been employed ; but is that to militate
against my character ? did I succeed by dishonourable means ? I dare not mention with
my own name, in point of talent and purity,
that great and innocent being—my dear Lord,
but upon my life, Mary, that man possessed
the wisdom of the serpent with the innocence
of the dove. He taught me, if I did not
think so before, that the most difficult things
might be accomplished by talent, wisdom, and
integrity."

We do not go further into details with which
the world is unconcerned, let it suffice that
Miss Ryder was convinced that she was loved—
that she loved in return—and month after

month passing away in vain attempts to persuade her family to acquiesce in her views, she
consented to be privately married to Dr. Scott
in London, in order to prevent the possibility
of their being ultimately separated in life.
Immediately after the ceremony she returned
to her father's house, where her engagement
remained a secret for some time. Her uncle,
Sir Richard Croft, alone was informed of it by
Dr. Scott himself, and he kindly did everything
in his power to reconcile the family to the
event. It was several weeks, however, before
this point could be even partially accomplished;
but on the 9th of July, 1807, they were re-
married at Hendon, and Mrs. Scott immediately
accompanied her husband into Essex.

Thus commenced their married life. They
resided at the vicarage house, at Burnham, a
village adjoining Southminster, the curacy of
which Dr. Scott held with his living. They
lived in perfect retirement, which their small
means rendered necessary ; for unlike admirals'

secretaries in general, he had saved no fortune;
but even with this precaution, and every other
economical effort—in which it is true the previous lives of neither had given them much
experience—they never could attain the comfort of independence; a painful situation for
one of Scott's refined feelings. " I never," he
once wrote to his wife, "regretted my fortunes
in life on my own account, but I do now on
yours !"

Oppressive as the constant sense of their
insufficient means must have been, with the
prospect of a family, (for in April, 1808, Mrs.
Scott became the mother of a girl, who was
duly christened Horatia, in accordance with
Lord Nelson's desire,) still their love knew no
diminution, and they read and talked, and
lived together, too much, perhaps, as if in
these delightful occupations were included all
the necessary realities of life. " We were a
couple of romantic fools," said Dr. Scott, in
speaking of this period, " and spent our days in

reading Italian poetry together." Mrs. Scott was also very fond of flowers, and had pursued the study of botany, and it was the pride of her husband to have her garden decorated with everything that was beautiful or rare that he could procure. What the world calls *management*, it may be feared neither of them possessed. Scott certainly did not, and in some of his letters to his wife during her absence from home, he mentions with a sort of ludicrous remorse, the expensive domestic catastrophes to which this deficiency gave rise.

TO MRS. SCOTT.

May, 1808, Tuesday night.

MY DEAR MARY,—Mrs. Beckwith sent her child yesterday to be named, and presently after sent to beg some beer, which I refused. Reflecting upon this, I took it into my head to inquire about our beer, of which we brewed six weeks ago, two hogsheads of 63 gallons each. To my astonishment, I found the second barrel was nearly gone. So that, in five weeks or thereabouts, we have drank 126 gallons of beer. You and I have not assisted; Ann and Sarah drink water, as they tell me. Keep all this to ourselves, for if your mother knew she would whip us. When finished, I shall leave them all without beer for a month or so. John works hard, and so does Harrington; quære, when I am out of the way?

TO MRS. SCOTT.

May 7th, 1808.
9 o'clock, Wednesday evening, in a fit of despair.

My dear Mary,—I am very miserable, and want you to make a dismal croak with me. I was flattering myself with a journey to London on Monday, in *our gig*, with Nonsuch. Half an hour since Bayley come to borrow the gig to go to Chelmsford to-morrow. It was put in the barn out of the way some time ago by James, lo and behold, we have discovered one of the *shafts broken in twain*. I have questioned

every one, but nobody knows. Now you are
to understand it was the strongest piece of
manufacture my eyes ever beheld; it never
could have been broke unknown t o any one.
I can only have an additional reason to be
glad of James being gone. If I still remain in
the hands of the Philistines, I shall not, at all
events, suffer from his carelessness. It is a
rascally piece of business, but I say no more
about it. * * * Interest sways every one I fear
in this world, unless some odd out-of-the-way
creatures like you and me.

Other instances might be given, but enough
has been said of such familiar anecdotes. Ever
sanguine as to results, Scott persisted in farming
in the face of continued losses, and still hoped
against hope in regard to preferment. His old
friend Sir Hyde Parker died, and to his surprise, he found a living on his estate in Suffolk,
of which he had every expectation of the next
presentation, was not settled on him. It was

a small vicarage, as described by Sir Hyde
Parker, "which should you think worth your
acceptance, you undoubtedly have the first
claim for; a neat parsonage, and the church
within a hundred yards of the mansion. This
may not be a bad retreat after your return
from Jamaica, during the autumn and fall of
the year." A specific arrangement for a living
in Bedfordshire had been made by his uncle,
Admiral Scott, with Mr. Michael Angelo Taylor,
but this also slipped through his hands. He
was in town occasionally with his friends, who
were connected with the government, and were
still desirous of serving him, but the opportunity to do so never came. He bore all his
disappointments with that buoyancy and good
humour which were natural to him, and in the
prospect of a better living, of which the incum-
bent was then seventy years old, he playfully
consoled himself with the well-known joke, " I
am sure I do not wish for his death, but *his*
living."

The biographer of Dr. Scott, would fain not dwell upon the four brief years of his married life; sickness and sorrow so soon overshadowed them. First, came alarming symptoms in the old wounds Scott had received in the Topaz, which compelled him to stay in London some weeks, undergoing surgical treatment. Violent swelling in the mouth, accompanied by pain, for a while perfectly confounded the faculty, till at length, an exfoliation of the bone of the upper jaw took place, and after this painful and distressing process was over, his health and strength much improved, and his face was far less disfigured than might have been expected. His flesh and colour also returned to their natural appearance. This was in the autumn of 1809. In the spring of that year, Mrs. Scott was confined of another daughter, and in the year following, of a boy, who when nearly four months old, was unhappily lost, from the carelessness of a nurse, who overlaid him. At this time, Mrs. Scott was with her family, for

the purpose of consulting medical advice for
her own health, which had visibly declined
between the birth of her daughter Margaret,
and that of her last child, the little boy. Repeated attacks of what were called cold chills
in Essex, had weakened her greatly, and she
was also liable to internal spasms. She left
her baby when six weeks old, and was brought
to London for advice. Drs. Baillie and Denman,
as well as her uncle, Sir Richard Croft, saw her
constantly and were equally puzzled by her
symptoms; and at last, they consulted Dr. Pem-
berton, but in vain. As early as in June, 1811,
Mrs. Scott evidently felt her case to be hopeless. "I do not think I shall be long with
you," she says in writing to her husband; "nor
would the thought be much pain, were it not
for my poor babies. You will love them I
think, and remember the promise you have so
often made me, of not parting with them. God
Almighty bless you;" she adds, in concluding
her letter, "and reward you for the faith and

tenderness you have shown me. There is no human being, that possesses anything like the affection I bear you and our children." She continued at her father's house at Hendon, constantly visited by Dr. Scott, as he found opportunities to leave his parish. On the last Sunday she ever lived, supported in bed, by her aunt Miss Croft, she wrote a short letter, conjuring him to come to her immediately, instead of on the following Tuesday, as had been expected. In this, she expressed her full sense of her danger, but the letter never reached Dr. Scott, as the express passed him on the road, and he arrived about noon on Monday, of his own accord. Though he had thus anxiously hastened to her bedside, the first moment he was released from his duties, he could not be persuaded that the attack was anything more than he had frequently witnessed; and in this delusion, he remained until the early part of Tuesday morning, when he found in her room, a phial containing quicksilver; and on being told, that

M

this had been administered without effect, he
gave himself instantly up to despair of her
recovery.   She took leave of her two little girls
with perfect composure and resignation, about
an hour before her death, saying to Miss Croft,
" Take them away now, aunt, for I shall meet
them again."   Towards Dr. Scott she was peculiarly tender and energetic, urging him, for
the sake of his children to marry again, and
even pointing out his cousin Miss Cutler.   The
pain and sickness ceasing, as mortification came
on, she took leave of all her family, and sighed
away her life, on Tuesday, the 20th of September, her twenty-sixth birth-day.

Her husband and brothers followed her to
the grave, and poor Dr. Scott would have fallen
into it himself, had they not supported him.
Her children never mentioned her, even when
their mourning was put on, as if they had
really meant to spare the feelings of others.
Horatia said, on passing the first time through
the room and looking at the bed, " Ah ! I

thought so." Several months afterwards, when
they were going home with their father, Margaret was heard to say to her sister, " I am glad
we are going to Burnham home, Horatia, for
then, we shall see our mamma, and brother
George." Horatia answered, " No, I don't
think we shall, Margaret, for I think mamma
is gone right away."

Thus painfully and suddenly terminated the
brief period of Dr. Scott's married happiness.
Mr. Rose, in writing to him on the occasion of his
bereavement, says, " I do not attempt to offer
you any consolation on the irretrievable loss
you have sustained, because it would be imper-
tinent to do so. Resignation to the will of
Providence, is the only resource in all such
cases." To this, Scott piously submitted
himself.

His life may now be said to have lost all its
adventure, but other interests arose to occupy
his mind, and to these he energetically devoted
his best powers. In all the duties of a parish

priest, he exerted himself unweariedly for the improvement of the two parishes under his charge; so much so, as even to draw forth the commendations of his diocesan, both by public testimonial, and incidental observation. The former appears in a letter from the Bishop of London, (now Archbishop of Canterbury,) to the secretary of the National Society, writ-ten soon after one of his lordship's pastoral visits to Southminster; and Lady Liverpool wrote to Dr. Scott as follows :

" I have lately seen the Bishop of London, who speaks of you most kindly, and with great praise. He has, indeed, done you full justice. How happy you must feel, when you reflect on the good you have done to your poor neigh-bours."

One of the chief ways in which he evinced his desire to benefit his parishioners, was by affording them more extended means of reli-gious education, which in this somewhat remote district had been much neglected ; and the poor

were consequently in a very ignorant and un-
cultivated state. It will be remembered, that
thirty years ago, the question of the education
of the poor was one, which although it had
begun to excite very general attention, was yet
much disputed. Dr. Scott, however, though
by no means a young man, and therefore un-
likely to be captivated by the mere novelties
of the day, held most decided opinions in favour
of the measure; and advocated it with a warmth
and devotion, worthy of the most zealous educa-
tionist of later times. Fragments of his ideas
on the plan of general instruction, show that he
had taken up the subject philosophically, and
with due reflection. " I consider," says he,
"that the intellectual power of a nation is
opposed to the physical force of it, just as the
spirit is opposed to the flesh, and that every
means should be used to strengthen the one,
in order to control the other. I believe that
so far from endangering the present gradations
of society, it would render them more stable,

and more worthy of being so. I admit, that
knowledge is power, and that if you give additional power to the lower classes, unless the
higher classes improve in knowledge also, it
will be endangering them. Well, then, all I can
say is, let them be so endangered, as the danger will rouse them to exert themselves, and
maintain their superiority by cultivating their
minds still more and more. What a desolate
waste of talent and leisure might then be
employed ! But if the poor people's minds
be cultivated, will they work ? Yes, for let the
rich improve themselves, and they will always
maintain their own position; and knowledge
when it ceases to be a distinction, will not make
the vulgar above the duties of their humble
sphere."

With these liberal notions, Dr. Scott strove
zealously to establish in his parish of Southminster, schools to be connected with the
National Society, in London; and for a while he
had to combat the opposition of prejudice, and

the difficulty of raising funds for the buildings
and endowment. But by his continued efforts
both these obstacles were gradually overcome,
and a few years after his first endeavours in the
cause, he had enlisted nearly the whole parish
in his favour, and had drawn the attention of the
Governors of the Charter-house so effectually
to the subject, that from its foundation to the
present time, they have been very munificent
patrons of the establishment. The first thing
accomplished was the building of a schoolroom
for 150 boys; the expense of which, amounting
to about £350, was defrayed by parish rates,
and the site was also given by the parish. The
school was opened on January 1, 1814, and in
a few weeks was attended by 124 boys, which
included every male child in the parish, capable of receiving instruction. The donations
and subscriptions for this year, amounted to a
very considerable sum, comprising a gift of £100
from the Charter-house, which with a similar
grant from the National Society, was employed
in erecting a girls' school, on the same scale as

the other. These schools, founded in a secluded
village, very soon had a most beneficial result
on the lower orders. Dissenters and absenters,
who (as Bishop Porteus reminded Dr. Scott on
his promotion to the living) existed in abundance
there, and had been gaining ground very fast,
received a strong check from the strict education in the doctrines and discipline of the
Church of England, which was enforced. This
was still further promoted by the interesting
and exact performance of divine service by the
vicar, who throughout his clerical life was remarkable for his impressive delivery, a point
which he had deeply studied himself, and which
he considered was far too little attended to,
generally, by the clergy in their preparation for
Holy Orders. His own scrupulous exactness
in all exterior observances had always been
noted, and gained for him in the Navy the
good-natured appellation of " high priest,"
and " old orthodox." Verily, as Lord Nelson
used to say of himself, " he loved the religion
transmitted to us by our forefathers."

By these and other good works, attention was more visibly drawn to religion. His own zeal kindled a fellow feeling in the minds of the parishioners; and his representations to the patrons of his benefice, so far procured their co-operation, that they subscribed annually £25 to his schools. The Bishop of London preached an anniversary sermon, which sustained public interest in the institutions, and they remain to this day, a pious monument of his benevolent activity.

He also rendered the greatest assistance to schools, already founded at Burnham, which were completely reformed by him. He filed a bill in Chancery, against the existing trustees, then added to their number, becoming one himself; and, by judicious management of the estates of the charity, increased their rental by more than £50 a year.

Throughout this period, the solitariness of his life, was increased by his regularly sending his little girls during the winter months, to

M 3

their grandmother in London, which place he
had himself entirely deserted, and was often
reproached by many of his friends there for
the life of seclusion he had adopted. He was
not, however, forgotten; the interest which
Lady Liverpool had felt in him and his family
remained unimpaired, and, in June 1816, Lord
Liverpool offered to recommend him to the
Prince Regent for the crown living of Catterick
in Yorkshire, which was then vacant. His
lordship represented it as having become in
value from £1,000 to £1,400 a year, in consequence of a decree lately obtained in the Exchequer ; and though he qualified this account
by avowing that he was not fully informed on
the subject, he added, in conclusion—" I certainly consider the living as one of the best in
the gift of the crown." Dr. Scott did not at
once accept it, for the first notion of his prede-
cessor having been encumbered with a long
and tedious lawsuit, naturally deterred him,
and he discovered too, that that gentleman had

died at Brussels the very day before the decree
was pronounced in his favour. He also found
the vicarage house in a very dilapidated state,
which, as the former vicar died insolvent, he
knew it would fall upon him to restore. These
facts made him pause, but, as he could obtain
no clear information of any intention on the
part of the tithe payers to resist the decision
of the Court of Exchequer, he at length accepted the living, which he afterwards frequently said, he never would have done, could
he have anticipated what followed. On preparing to reside in Yorkshire, to the sincere regret
of his parishioners in Essex, the inhabitants
of Burnham, with whom his connexion now
altogether ceased, presented him with a large
and beautiful silver salver, " upon his quitting
the curacy, as a small token of gratitude, for
many essential services, rendered them during
a residence of twelve years in their parish."

It may be mentioned here also, that his acquirements as one of the brotherhood of Free-

masons had been acknowledged by the lodge held at Burnham, by the present of a silver star, with all the appropriate mystical insignia upon it. He had been a mason from an early period in his sea-life, and held the highest opinions of the usefulness of the order, especially to all travellers in foreign countries.

Before quitting Southminster, he sent to his diocesan a valuable old book from his library, which the latter acknowledged to him thus kindly : " I shall value it chiefly as the memorial of a clergyman, whose labours I trust will long continue to benefit his late parishioners, and whose loss' I cannot but regret, for the sake of the diocese, though I sincerely rejoice that due attention has at length been paid to his merits and his claims."

It was necessary that Dr. Scott should have a chaplain's scarf as a legal qualification for holding two livings. He had been appointed one of the Prince of Wales's chaplains in 1801, and gazetted as such, but, upon claiming the

privilege, he found that, owing to the accidental
omission of one of his christian names, and
another trifling informality, this appointment
was not valid.   This difficulty was obviated by
his being made a king's chaplain in November,
1816.

CHAPTER XI.

Resides at Catterick—literary habits—education of his children—his library—opinion on Roman Catholic securities.

In the spring of the following year he took possession of the vicarage of Catterick ; and, from circumstances that will be detailed, retired more and more from the world, and into his library and his own thoughts—occupying himself also with his children, who were now attaining an age when education became necessary. It is remarkable that he had scarcely come into residence, before he was applied to by a mutual friend of Lord Nelson and himself for a small piece of preferment of which he was become patron, for a young clergyman who was engaged to be married to Miss Horatia Nelson. It would seem, however, that the benefice was

not vacant when the request was made. The
gross value of the living of Catterick, turned
out to be about half what had been represented.
It was found, too, that the decree which had
crowned the nine years' warfare of his prede-
cessor, was a dead letter, in consequence of
that gentleman's death, immediately before, as
has been mentioned, and Scott was therefore
compelled to begin the suit *de novo*. In 1819,
another decree was obtained in the vicar's
favour; on which the defendants appealed to
the House of Lords, but afterwards withdrew
their appeal, and submitted to the decree. It
was supposed that the whole affair was now
settled, as arrears, costs, &c. were paid by Dr.
Scott's opponents; but, notwithstanding this,
they afterwards set up certain moduses, thereby
weakening the force of the decree, and involving fresh suits, which continued for many
years after, and were never finally adjusted,
till the commutation of tithes took place in the
parish, the benefit of which Scott never lived
to enjoy.

We dwell no more on these harassing facts,
which certainly embittered many an hour in
this portion of his life, although it never interrupted his kind feeling, or the respect and good
will of his parishioners towards him. But he
retired into his home disheartened, to say the
least of it, at being forced into contest at an
age when years and the events he had survived
made peace and quietness so desirable to him.

His life may now be called a strictly studious
one.   His affection for books, and pleasure in
book-collecting seemed to increase rather than
otherwise ; an amusing instance of which occurred soon after his arrival at Catterick.

Among the various requisites for his new establishment was a horse, and, hearing of one
likely to suit him at Darlington, in the county
of Durham, he went thither with thirty pounds
in his pocket, determined on purchasing the
animal. When he arrived, however, he repaired, in the first instance, as was his custom,
to the principal bookseller's shop ; and that at

Darlington, as it happened, was stocked with old volumes of so rare and curious a kind that, before he left it, (the temptation being irresistible, and the horse forgotten,) he had spent every shilling of his money with the worthy bibliopole, and, on reaching home, created a sensation in his household, which involuntarily reminds one of Moses Primrose's return from the fair.

Among the literary amusements in which he now occupied himself, one of the first to which he was naturally led, was the investigation of the antiquities with which the place and neighbourhood abounded. Catterick, supposed to be an old Roman encampment, called Cataractonium, or Cataracton, afforded in itself a rich field for speculation, and he dissented from all former opinions as to the derivation of the name. It had usually been considered as derived from the word Cataract, which antiquaries were obliged to go to Richmond to discover in the fall of the Swale

there, but Dr. Scott imagined it to have a far
more ancient origin, and as some of his ingenious suggestions may be interesting to the
etymologist, we give an extract or two from
his memoranda.

" Hint for a British Antiquarian.

"Cataractonium, sive Cataracton, cannot have
any allusion to a cataract, but is probably the
name given to the place by the Romans, lati-
nizing by ear the ancient British name, whatever
it was. There is no cataract at Catterick, nor
any vestige of one; and to go to Richmond
for one to give name to the place, seems even
absurd. I hold that derivation to be a very
wild one. Looking at the *artificial mound* at
Catterick, I cannot help going farther back for
a derivation of its name. According to Bryant's
radicals, *Ca* signifies a place, *tor, tar,* a hill, or
artificial mound; and *uc* or *uch,* high. Cata-
ruch or Catterick, may have, in ancient times,
signified ' the place of the high hill,' the sacri-

ficial mound,' such as in early times were used for altars. For as Bryant says, ' the names of high mounds, promontories, hills and rivers, are of long duration.' Perhaps the mound at Catterick, evidently an artificial one, was a Puratheia, or place of fire worship ; as well as the artificial mounds of the Castle Hills, which latter may well be called μαστοειδεις λοφοι."

Another of his conjectures as to the derivation of the word was, that it signified " the place of going over," or a ford,—

Tha Thar } over, across Thair		Cathair { ford, or place (of going) over,

cathairich, to pass over, a bridge or ford. Hearing *some* such words, the Romans called the place Cataracton, or Cataractonium, for *tharich* is probably, ' to cause to pass over.' Catterick Bridge over the Swale, seems to corroborate this last idea.

The last twenty-two years of Dr. Scott's life were on the whole as uniform, as his previous life had been varied. His children were growing up under his eye, a constant source of interest and delight to him; and he revised and superintended the instruction he procured for them at home, carrying out while so doing, some of his favourite theories on education. One of these was the teaching the Latin, instead of the English Grammar; and the consequence of this introduction to the Classics was that his elder daughter pursued them to some extent. The entry in his journal for March 28, 1821, is, "The children have now been thrice through the fourteen rules of Dr. Russell's Charterhouse Grammar." His rooms in the vicarage, at Catterick, were entirely surrounded with books, all of which he had more or less read, and it was his great pride to see his children's interest drawn to them, and especially to the study of languages; a pursuit which he resumed himself from time to time, with undiminished ardour.

His own acquirements sat so lightly upon

him, that it was not possible for him to com-
municate them to others in a dull or ponderous
form. They had been desultorily although
industriously prosecuted by himself; and he
had no notion of forcing them upon others, so
that any proficiency which his children made
as linguists was chiefly spontaneous, the fruits
of inheritance and example, and the natural
result of living in an atmosphere of foreign
books. In saying that the rooms were surrounded with books, it must not be supposed
that these were confined to the sitting apartments. Every bedroom had its share, perhaps
some of them more than their share of volumes;
and the house contained a long gallery, the
whole of one side of which was also furnished
with well-stocked shelves. Of the contents of
this voluminous library, which, except in Divinity, was but scantily supplied with English
works, it is difficult to give a just idea. But,
perhaps, there never was a private library of
the same size, in which were books of such

varied reference and in so many languages,
brought together. A cursory glance at the
catalogue, discovers dictionaries and grammars
alone, for about forty different tongues. The
affection which their owner cherished for these
books, collected with so much pains, and during
a series of so many years; dragged too from
one end of the world to the other, and necessarily connected with scenes and interests never
to be forgotten; became a strong feature in
his character, and invested him with an eccen-
tric charm, in the eyes of many who had the
opportunity of appreciating him. His habits
of application and study never forsook him at
Catterick. He might have been seen there
day after day, and evening after evening, poring
over some favourite folio; or making extracts
in his large upright hand, interrupting himself
occasionally by getting up to walk quarter-deck
as he called it, talking half audibly to himself
in the earnestness of his thoughts, and perfectly
abstracted from every thing that was passing

around him, all which traits of his habits at
that time, will be easily recognised by those
who knew him. He enjoyed nothing more
than exhibiting his library, whenever he could
find a kindred spirit, and the gratification he
experienced in once showing his treasures to
Dr. Parr, who was an accidental visitor at his
house, will be long remembered by those who
witnessed it.

To the latest day of his life his love of book-
collecting continued. "It appears very clearly,"
says a literary gentleman, in writing to him,
" that you have either undergone inoculation,
or taken the disease naturally; which of the
two is not very easy to divine, and are now
very near the feverish meridian of bibliomania-
cism." There was nothing feverish, however,
in the enjoyment which he had in his researches
at the bookstalls in London, during his occasional visits there. On the contrary, he settled
down at an old stall, comfortably and patiently
as Isaac Walton on the bank of one of his fa-

vourite streams, and so often would he visit and
revisit them whenever he had the opportunity,
that some of the bookstall keepers in the neighbourhood of Holborn can scarcely fail to remember a venerable looking old gentleman with
white hair, in a shovel hat and loose great
coat, standing, in calm satisfaction for perhaps
half an hour, or more, conning through his
spectacles volume after volume, and at last
going in to cheapen his purchases, for an old
book was a thing he always bargained for.
Thus it was that, maintaining a deep interest
in his library, studying intensely the earlier
divines of our church, and our controversy with
Rome, and, subsequently, a complicated law
investigation of the rights to tithes from certain marsh lands in his parish in Essex, he
lived exclusively in the days and years which
were gliding over, and the circumstances of his
earlier life became for the most part as a
dream that was gone.

His sea adventures were seldom mentioned,

even to his own family—his neighbours were
unaccustomed to regard him, except historically,
as Nelson's chaplain ; and when the past was
revived, it was ever reluctantly, and with pain
to himself. Perhaps it was well that the past
did become a dream to him—one who had felt
so tenderly, that he could not to the last recall
the loss of those he had loved without the keen
emotion of recently wounded feelings, was fortunate in possessing a mind sufficiently active for
his thoughts and interests to be led into other
channels. They were so led, and the employé of
heroes became insensibly transformed into the
musing antiquarian, and retired parish priest.

But there was one subject which for a time
effectually roused him from his seclusion. In
the discussions on the emancipation of the Roman Catholics, before the passing of the bill in
1829, he became warmly interested, and took an
active part. His views were peculiar, neither
on the one hand, regarding an alliance with
Rome as essentially unholy on account of her

N

errors in doctrine; nor, on the other, considering
the question as merely political, and separable
from the laws and genius of Romanism. And
these views we record as his firm and lasting
opinions upon a topic which is still most important, and one which few but those as deeply
learned as himself, have had the opportunity of
looking at on every side.

In 1828, a meeting was held at Richmond, in
Yorkshire, to consider the agitated measure of
emancipation; on which occasion Dr. Scott
broke through his ordinary habits, and spoke
as follows :

" I am no exclusionist, and in saying so, I
trust my sentiments are directly in accordance
with those of Lord Eldon, the Duke of Wellington, and the whole bench of bishops, and
with them I strongly deprecate the admission
of our brethren of the church of Rome to political power, while they continue to maintain,
in discipline and morals, principles, not merely
adverse, but actively hostile to those of all other
churches of our common Christianity.   When

such securities are given, as shall secure church
and state, then, and not till then, I shall be
ready to grant what is called emancipation ;
and, in saying so, I do not speak jesuitically,
for, if I thought, like many others, that no security could be found out, I should not disguise
my sentiments. But I do believe securities can
be afforded ; and, when that difficulty is got
the better of, I shall hail with pleasure my
Roman Catholic brethren as fellow citizens, in
full and equal enjoyment of civil power with
myself. The securities, however, must be
given by them, not taken by us, so as to
render the object safely attainable, without
offending the conscientious scruples of our
brethren ;—that is, without in the least inter-
fering with the purely theological Roman Catholic faith, to interfere with which, or to
speak reproachfully of which, I should hold to
be an insult, while such a point as emancipation is at issue. I maintain that the participa-
tion of civil power might be fully granted to

Roman Catholics, provided the hierarchy of
the church of Rome would do away with their
intolerable canons, the penal statutes I may
call them of the discipline of their church,
which, while they exist in force, must for ever
render Romanists decidedly and actively hostile to every mode of Christian faith and form
of worship but their own. The purely theological faith of the Roman Catholic church,
however different from our own, is one thing;
the code of morals and discipline deduced from
it is another; and it is against the latter as to
many of its present tenets that I protest; nor,
until a reformation of them takes place, can we
ever accede to their wishes. There is, indeed,
no competent power to alter, change, or abro-
gate any one article of the theological faith and
doctrine of the Roman Catholic church, as to
which, not even the pope is able, directly or
indirectly, to grant a dispensation, although, as
to morals and discipline, he can dispense with
or modify them as he pleases, insomuch that
the objectionable and deadly hostile canons of

discipline might be done away with, without
intrenching upon the rights of conscience, if
the pope and hierarchy of the church of Rome
would grant that blessing to all spiritual subjects in the British isles. For example, the
celibacy of the clergy—prayers in the Latin
tongue—and the denial of the cup to the laity,
are not articles of purely theological faith, but
of discipline; and the pope might grant the
cup to the laity—permit the marriage of his
clergy—and allow the Roman church service
to be celebrated in the vulgar tongue. In the
same manner he might do away with the obnoxious canons and decrees to which 1 have
alluded; the abrogation of which would free
the whole English Roman Catholic Christian
flock from their present thraldom, and it
would be no longer necessary to keep up such
a barrier of defence as the making the denial
of transubstantiation a test for admission to
civil power, to which test our ancestors were
driven by the preposterous and cruel canons of
the Roman code, so dangerous in principle to

our English church and state, and drawn up as
it were in hostile array against them both.
Let then, the competent authority which exists
in the Roman Catholic church government
concede such spiritual emancipation to its subjects in this country by the suspension, dero-
gating from, or complete abrogation of the
obnoxious decrees and canons. The moment
that is done, the necessity for exclusion ceases.
But until they are done away with, no possible
security can be given by Roman Catholics for
the security of our church establishment, but
such as to be effectual must interfere with their
rights of conscience. The pope's dispensing
power rendering all other securities not worth
a straw."

An explanation of the opinions which are
succinctly stated in this speech, has been most
kindly afforded by a clergyman* in the vicinity
of Catterick, to whom Dr. Scott frequently and
fully expressed his sentiments, and who was no

* The Rev. George Townsend, Prebendary of Durham, &c. &c.

less interested than himself in the exciting debates of the day. This friend's account of them is as follows:—

" Dr. Scott considered the one great error of the church of Rome to be, the confounding together the canons which relate to discipline, with the conclusions which relate to faith, and so making two entirely distinct things articles of the creed, or propositions essential to salvation. The first article of the creed of Pope Pius, which is generally called the Creed of the Council of Trent, requires the member of the church of Rome to receive an undefined and undefinable mass of observances. The 11th declares the church of Rome to be supreme over other churches; and the 12th article demands his adherence to all the canons of all the general councils.

" The intermediate articles refer to the sacraments, justification, transubstantiation, purgatory, the saints, and images.

" Now it is evident that a Christian may be-

lieve in transubstantiation, and still be a good
legislator, provided he does not endeavour to
make his peculiar opinions the faith of the
community, by changing the law, and requiring
the subject to receive his notions, or become
amenable to a civil tribunal.   A man may believe or disbelieve that his soul will or will not
pass to heaven through purgatory, and still
make a good admiral, general, judge, and magistrate.   This, however, is not the question.
The question is, whether our duty to God is
not, or ought not always in all cases to be superior to our duty to man.   All sects, churches,
and individuals who believe in the immortality
of the soul, and in the immortal results therefore, which follow obedience to the dictates of
conscience, will unanimously declare that God
must be served and not man.   First God, then
Cæsar, is the rule of him who gave the common
gospel both to Rome, England, and the world.
But now the controversy begins.   The question is, what is our duty to God?   That alone

is our duty to God which we are convinced
from the study of his own gospel to be the
rule of our conduct.   The church of Rome
teaches its people that the bishop of that
church, possesses by the authority, command,
and positive injunction of the law of God, some
power, not capable of accurate definition, over
all other bishops and churches.   The mode
and form in which this power is to be exercised,
is contained in the canons of councils, which
the Council of Trent has prevented from being
mutable by having made them articles of faith.
If, therefore, a nation which desires to be in
union even with Rome, discovers in those
canons any matters which it deems to be incon-
sistent with its own duty to God, or with the
happiness of the people, and if it then says to
Rome, ' We do not wish to separate from you,
and we object not to your faith, but to your
laws of discipline, and we will give you all
privileges among us, if you will rescind those
canons or laws;'   the church of Rome is now

compelled to answer, 'We have made every
canon of every general council a portion of our
articles of faith, required by the law of God,
and forming a part therefore of our duty to God,
and we cannot depart from this faith.' 'But,'
says the independent nation or people in reply,
'we read in these canons which form a part
of your faith, that if we do not adopt all your
conclusions, you call us heretics, and declare
that you have authority from God to punish
heretics, and a part of that punishment is to
inflict great political evils upon a state, by
requiring and commanding other nations to
obey their God by punishing with invasion the
people that will not obey you; this is your
claim—it was once influential, it has now,
apparently, ceased to be so. Because of this
cessation, you demand us not to examine into
the claim you make, but to give you the same
privileges with those who make no such claim.
If it is obsolete, rescind it.' 'Oh, no!' says
the church of Rome, 'though it seems to
be obsolete, it still remains a matter of

faith, and therefore a point of duty to God: and we prefer God to man, Christ to Cæsar. We will not rescind, and yet we demand the power to legislate in your councils.'

"What then is to be done ? Both parties are at a dead lock. ' This may be done,' says Dr. Scott. ' Let the church of Rome separate her canons of discipline from her articles of faith. If Rome will do this, Rome can give securities to a Protestant government, and the members of its church may be safely admitted to power. The common laws of toleration demand that opinions should be free. The common laws of political safety require that the liberty of the people be not injured by foreign pretensions. We will tolerate your opinions, but we will secure our people's liberty. Both objects will be accomplished by your giving this security. Separate your faith from your discipline; change the latter. Demand no power over those whom you are pleased to call heretics. Govern your own people by your own canons : do not govern us. By a council, by your pope,

by your college of cardinals, or by whatever
authority it may be, which rules your church,
rescind the identity of the canons which we
call persecuting, from the faith we call erro-
neous, and you may keep all your errors, and
we will not suspect your loyalty, your patriotism,
or your good intentions.   Give us this security,
and you shall no longer be excluded from
power.'   Such was Dr. Scott's reasoning.   His
knowledge of the canon law, his experience of
the world, his frequent conversations with
Spanish priests and gentlemen in Spain, who
agreed with him in the difference betwen the
old catholicism of antiquity, when Rome was
regarded as the first of the equal churches, and
the modern catholicism in which Rome calls
itself the first, not in precedency only, but
in supremacy, all confirmed him in these views.

"Very delightful," adds Mr. Townsend'
"were the animating and interesting conversations which I was accustomed to hold
with Dr. Scott on these topics.   There was
no man among all my circle of acquaintance,

and that will include many deeply learned
and well-read people, whose knowledge of this
great controversy was equal to that of Dr.
Scott. I loved him for his amiable and gentle
character, I prized his friendship, I admired
his learning, and some of the happiest hours
of my life were those which he passed with
me at Northallerton, and which I passed with
him at Catterick."

Mr. Townsend regretted, when he afforded
this valuable record of Dr. Scott's opinions,
that he had mislaid memoranda, in which the
latter had laid down the distinction from the
canon law between canones, dogmata, doctrinæ,
leges, and articuli fidei. " He had there shown,"
says Mr. Townsend, " how they were originally
distinguished from each other, and how the
church of Rome hastily, unadvisedly, and most
unjustifiably and uncanonically, confused and
amalgamated them together."

CHAPTER XII.

Disappointed in Catterick—letters—friends—goes to Southminster—daughter's marriage—illness—Ecclesfield—death
—concluding remarks.

DR. SCOTT seldom went to London.   The occasions of his doing so were, for the most part
either to perform his duty at the Chapel Royal,
or to visit his parish of Southminster.   On one
of the former occasions, soon after the accession
of King William IVth, his majesty's reception
of him at the next levée was so kind, recognis-
ing him as Lord Nelson's chaplain, stepping
out of the circle, and graciously extending his
hand, as he thanked him for his " most excellent sermon," that he had again very serious
thoughts of applying to government, on the
fact of his disappointment in the value of his

Yorkshire living, and drew up a memorial to the King to that effect, praying for some other preferment, more compatible with his ease and comfort, when he would most willingly resign Catterick. But he shrunk from presenting his address, for he had at all times little heart for begging, and, " still he bore it with a patient shrug."

And so he lived on at Catterick, universally known and respected. Indeed, the regard which he excited amongst his friends gene-rally, was that of cordial affection, and this may probably have been a little heightened by the events of his early life, although, as we have said, they were seldom mentioned. Cir-cumstances, nevertheless, did sometimes re-vive them, as will be seen by the following hearty extract from a letter of the Rev. James Tate, canon of St. Paul's.

TO THE REV. DR. SCOTT.

Portsmouth, 5th September, 1834.

MY DEAR OLD FRIEND,—Whatever excuse I

might invent for having been two months at
Portsmouth, and never dropped a line to Catterick, to say that I was tasting new modes of
existence connected with frequent reminiscences
of Dr. Scott, whatever excuse I could *else* invent
might serve till yesterday morning, possibly,
but not over yesterday afternoon. Where do
you think we all were yesterday? From the
sally port, under the command of my gallant
nephew, Lieut. Campbell of Marines, we all,
(nine formed the party,) took a boat up the
harbour, with the pious purpose of visiting as
pilgrims, your old ship, the Victory, and won-
derfully delighted we were (the tyros of our
company) with the interior sights of that city
of wood. A full hour or more was soon con-
sumed in wanderings along all the decks, even
down to the water ·tanks at the bottom of all.
The very spot marked with a brass plate, " England expects," &c. on which your friend the
hero got his mortal wound, and the room now
kept sacred, part of the cockpit, or close by it,

in which he expired—received due contemplation.   *   *   *   *

Several weeks ago I got a sight of the dock yard at Portsmouth, and shook hands with your hero's favourite sailing master (he is now master attendant in the yard) Atkinson from Gilling.*   He is a fine, hearty old fellow, and enjoys apparently such recollections with great zest.

Before the close of this month, we all hope to be fairly settled once more within the sound of St. Paul's great bell.   Next month brings round my periodical duties as canon residentiary.   God bless you, my dear friend, and all whom you love.

Ever yours,

JAMES TATE.

We quote also a letter from the Rev. George Townsend, not only for the strong regards it breathes towards Dr. Scott, but for the additional

* Gilling is a village a few miles from Catterick.

testimony it affords to his great learning and
experience.

College, Durham, 11th April, 1838.

MY DEAR DR. SCOTT,—I send you a letter
missive of inquiry, friendship, and reminis-
cence, though I have nothing very particular
to say to you, except that I wish I could induce
you in the course of the spring or summer, to
visit me at Durham.   In looking over this
morning, some old memoranda and letters, I
found three or four very kind and affectionate
notes from you, and they made me wish I
knew more of you, and that we had more intimate association together.   Much intimacy,
however, unless with identity of pursuit, taste,
and bias, and when persons are living near
each other, is almost impossible in the present
state of society.   I have often regretted that
you have never written, in a connected trea-
tise, the results of your extensive reading in

ecclesiastical matters, as compared with your own observations in your residence in Spain, and in the southern countries of Europe.

*   *   *   *   *

I hope you will forgive this gossiping letter, and, with kind remembrances to all,

Believe me, my dear Dr. Scott,

Faithfully and truly yours,

GEORGE TOWNSEND.

To the regret of the many friends who would have rejoiced in his society, Dr. Scott went but little from home, and, latterly, found his chief relaxation in the unlimited hospitality of his friends and parishioners, the Earl and Countess of Tyrconnel, at whose house at Kiplin he enjoyed for many years with his daughters, every comfort which the utmost kindness of sincere attachment could suggest. There was at Kiplin a valuable English library, which was a constant source of gratification to him, and, with the privilege of old age, he was so entirely at liberty to do what he liked, that he had all the enjoyment and independence of home, without the extreme seclusion to which he gave himself up at his own vicarage.

Seldom as it was that any thing occurred to remind him of his past life, he was yet occasionally present at a festival held yearly at the house of the late Captain Cumby, R.N., to commemorate the battle of Trafalgar, a merry meeting, attended by as many old Trafalgar men as could be assembled together; but, like all other anniversaries, it brought its melancholy associations, rarely did the same party twice meet; and before Dr. Scott was gone, the kind host himself had passed away.

In the spring of 1839, Dr. Scott arrived in London, with his younger daughter, and, leaving her on a visit with his old friends Lord Chief Justice Tindal, and his family, proceeded into Essex. In the July following, he returned to London, to be present at his daughter's marriage. In the interval, he had been preparing the vicarage house, at Southminster, intending that she and her husband should reside there, but events arose which prevented this, and he was left incumbered with the duties of his parish. An unfortunate circumstance, as, from his age and declining health, he was quite unable to fulfil the task. Unhappily also, the scrupulous conscientiousness he had always exercised in his appointments to the curacy of Southminster, now combined with irresolution of mind (consequent on his increasing bodily weakness) to prevent his disentangling himself from the difficulty. He continued to perform the duty far beyond the stretch of his powers, until, on one occasion, during divine service, the use of speech was entirely suspended. For months even, after this, he remained in the house, unfurnished as it was, with scarcely half a dozen books about him, and with harassing anxieties, accumulating from various causes, which were aggravated by his inability to attend to his affairs. Having,

throughout life, managed these in his own way,
he was jealous of interference. They now wore
on his spirits, and irritated his nerves, until
serious illness was produced, when, with much
difficulty, he was persuaded to leave his forlorn
and embarrassing situation, and repair to the
house of his-son-in law in Yorkshire. It was
quite evident to all who saw him, as he passed
through London, that he was " breaking up."
He was conscious of it himself, and was only
anxious to be spared to see his daughter Margaret again, and her infant —Miss Scott having
been with him for some time—and to reach his
own home at Catterick, the fittest place, as he
thought, for the event he felt approaching.
Though decidedly better than when he left
Essex, his appearance, when he arrived at Ecclesfield, was so altered and emaciated, that the
effect of one year was more like that of twenty,
he looked so extremely old as well as ill. The
most painful symptom of his malady was difficulty of respiration ; this, however, abated as

his mind grew more composed, and the weather, during the latter end of June, being
genial and reviving, contributed to relieve him.
Indeed, for many days, he was so much better,
that we had hopes that, after resigning altogether the duties at both his livings, he might
return from Catterick, and spend the remainder
of his life with us. This comfort, however, was
not permitted. On the night of the 23rd of
July, a violent paroxysm of his complaint came
on, which, instead of subsiding on the application of medicine, as it had hitherto done, continued to increase, and, on the arrival of the
doctor, his case was pronounced hopeless. That
poor Dr. Scott felt this himself was also evident,
for, on taking some medicine at the earnest
entreaty of those around him, he said, " It is
of no use—nothing but God and our Saviour
can do me any good now."

He bore his last sufferings, which were great,
with entire meekness and resignation, so much
so, as to affect the attendants who nursed him,

in a very unusual degree. Every little act of
care was so benevolently acknowledged, every
slight alleviation in his pain left him so calm
and gentle, kindly inquiring after his little
grandchild, and, by his manner, seeming anxious to cheer the sorrowing witnesses of his
state, that the warm affection of his nature was
never more touchingly displayed. Nothing
could be more impressive—nothing could be
more consoling—for nothing could be more
exemplary, than his departure from this life.
He asked the prayers of his family, and gave
them his own blessing, and, after several hours
of dozing, during which all pain had ceased,
he expired on the night of the 24th of July,
1840, just as midnight had turned, and so
quietly, that those who were watching only
knew of the event by his not breathing again.
He had completed his 72nd year, only the day
before.

To the last he retained his faculties, memory,
and all that susceptibility of mind which had

been the ornament of his earlier years. A few days before he died, he related several anecdotes of his youth previously unknown, which almost suggested the present little tribute to his memory. On the same morning he was conversing upon Sir Walter Scott's novels, and taking down a volume of the Pirate, it opened at Cleveland's noble "fragment of a sea ditty."

" Farewell, farewell, the voice you hear,
Has left its last soft tone with you."*

This he began to read aloud, when the allusions it contained, seemed to strike so forcibly on some mysterious chord within, that he became much agitated, but persisted in reading it through, which he did with the most touching pathos, until he laid down the book in tears.

This sensibility to poetry, had, indeed, never

* The Pirate, Vol. II., page 56, new edit., 1829.

deserted him in his old age. What can be more
charming than to imagine the Septuagenarian,
sitting down as he one day did at Catterick, to
write an epitaph for the gravestone of two favourite servants, who had died in his house and
lay buried in his churchyard ? It was a private
indulgence of feeling, and the scrap of paper
on which the lines were written, was not found
till after his death.

> Near to each other, now two clods of earth,
> Two friends of humble life lie buried here ;
> Regretted and lamented for their worth,
> Their faithful service, and their love sincere.
> What more than this can grateful memory say,
> They lived, they served, served well and pass'd away.

A second stanza, alluding to the higher service they had entered upon above, was left
unfinished.

His affection for music continued throughout
his life, occasionally he would himself strike
on the keys of the pianoforte, some of the wild
foreign airs which floated in his memory ; and

the vision of him is now before us, as when
animated by the playing of his daughters,
he would tread the well-remembered slow flat-
footed walz of Germany, in his own drawing
room. Sometimes his active thoughts would
interest themselves over a novel for the whole
evening, and even through the night if necessary, and the last volume had not been pur-
posely mislaid by his children; and this intensity
of application and interest would not be called
forth alone by the beautiful romances of Walter
Scott, or the absorbing horrors of Mrs. Rad-
cliffe, but the most ephemeral trash that ever
issued from the Minerva Press, could for the
time, chain him in abstraction; although his
feeling after reading any inferior work of fiction,
was to complain with a sort of shamefacedness,
that such books had been thrown in his way.
But it was the nature of his mind to lay hold
of any subject very strongly, and among other
instances of this, whenever he met a brother
chess player (in which game he was himself a

proficient) the interest became so painful, that, in later years, he never pursued the amusement. But let not these peculiarities impress the reader with the idea of a man who could not join in the light conversation or pastime of the hour.   Oh, no! a more pleasant companion, a more thorough-bred gentleman, a person more accessible to all ranks and all ages cannot be imagined, and on this account perhaps it is, we should say, that the impression of his superior powers and attainments, was most striking on a first interview, for being so thoroughly genial in disposition, you lost as you became acquainted with him, that sense of your own inferiority with which great talents sometimes never cease to burden you.   We should say, too, that, in both his habit of mind and manner in society, the advantage he had derived from intercourse abroad was very great.   He was one of the few people, perhaps, who appropriate all the good points of character in foreigners,— their freedom from prejudice and pride—their

general affability and courteous politeness—
(doing away with some of the harsher national
traits of John Bull,) without becoming tainted
by either their vanities or their vices.   This
result it was which, gilding the more essential
excellences of his moral being, made him immediately popular and beloved at every period
of his life.

The personal exterior of Dr. Scott was very
remarkable, his forehead was singularly fine
and intellectual, and the benevolent expression of his countenance and eyes, did justice to the universal kindness of his feelings.
He had looked much older than his time of
life warranted, ever since his wound in 1801 ;
but as this appearance of age became natural
with his advancing years, it assumed a most
reverend and even apostolic character.   A very
strong impression was made by it only a few
days before his death, when he accompanied
his son-in-law to an annual meeting of the

parish schools, in the village of Ecclesfield. He had wandered into the crowd, and was standing in the midst of the assembled children, when they sang their hymn. All eyes were attracted to his figure, his hat was off, his white hair unusually long and naturally waved, was moved in the wind, and the bright sunshine gleamed upon it, giving him, as he leaned upon his stick and looked up to heaven, a half spiritualized appearance.

His mortal remains were interred in a vault' in Ecclesfield churchyard, on the 31st day of July, 1840.

Thus was this excellent man altogether lost for this world, to those who loved and revered him. Though he had been permitted to survive the allotted measure of human existence, so much to the last was he capable of sharing in, and enjoying the pursuits and pleasures of his own family, that he was missed and lamented by them as a friend and companion. In him

his children lost the most affectionate and
devoted of parents; his servants the kindest
and most considerate of masters.   His home
had been a region in which all things had a
claim upon his heart.   Even the domestic
animal that lay at his foot, was an object of his
tender notice, and every article around formed
a part of the Lares. In Catterick, he is remembered for a benevolence of disposition, and
liberality of hand, which endeared him to his
parishioners throughout their intercourse; the
impression of which on many, will perhaps
never be effaced.   His piety was sincere, and
fervent as unostentatious. Among his friends
he was deplored with affectionate sorrow, nor
can we better illustrate the opinion generally
entertained of him, than by quoting the words
of Lord Chief Justice Tindal, on the occasion
of his death; who, after expressing "the sincerity with which he grieved for his departure,"
adds, " So much acquired learning, such good-

ness of heart, and such integrity of purpose, united in one man, can seldom be met with amongst his survivors, and the loss of those amiable and useful qualities create a regret amongst his friends, which it will require a length of time to forget."

APPENDIX.

TRANSLATION OF THE SARDINIAN

POEM ON TIME.

Oh wherefore dost thou not return again,
Time past and wasted, time bestow'd in vain ?

I.

Oh precious Time, oh Time too quickly flown,
Return, again return, and be mine own !
Thou Time, who art a God in power and worth,
To all the virtuous children of the earth ;
Thou Time, too late esteem'd by me, who now
In agony of grief before thee bow,
How blest, how useful hadst thou been to me,
Oh Time, if I in time had valued thee !
Then wherefore dost thou not return again,
Time past and wasted, Time bestow'd in vain ?

II.

Thou, who in constant motion dost maintain
All thy stability, return again !
Come back for me, for on my soul did lie
A heavy sleep, while thou wert passing by,
Thy whole existence, and thy very peace
Consist in motion that can never cease ;
Oh then return to me, Time ill employ'd,
And henceforth not a moment shall be void.
Oh wherefore, &c.

III.

Time, in the appointed measure of whose flight,
The sphere goes round, revolving day and night,
Have pity on my grief, restore me here,
To the beginning of my brief career,
From life's last season now upon the wing,
Restore me, oh restore me to its spring,
To be what once I was, wilt thou deny,
When all my life has fled unheeded by ?
Oh wherefore, &c.

IV.

The naked tree, of flowers and leaves deprived,
When May returns, has all its charms revived ;
And on the wither'd plains again appear,
The joyous colours of the opening year ;
Proud o'er the banks the river floods arise,
Which summer sunshine to a streamlet dries ;
But in the grey-hair'd man, by age subdued,
His early strength can never be renew'd.
Oh wherefore, &c.

V.

The aged serpent, from its skin decay'd,
Comes forth in pristine beauty rearray'd,
When the cold season yields to summer's prime ;
And the famed Phœnix of the eastern clime
Is born again, and with such vigour springs,
That agile as before she spreads her wings ;
But the immortal soul must ne'er behold
Her worn-out frame restor'd her, as of old :
Oh wherefore, &c.

VI.

'Tis true, at night's approach, day darkens round
When the sun dies upon the western bound,
But all returns to light, and shadow ends,
When newborn in the east he reascends ;
And the white moon, his sister, from the wane,
To her full splendour aye returns again ;
But man, once fallen from his high estate,
No earthly power can ever renovate.
Oh wherefore, &c.

VII.

Fear not, oh Time beloved, to be imbroil'd
In treacherous arts—imaginations wild—
In cobweb snares, in actions or in ways
Which reason and good sense alike dispraise,
In fancies, madnesses, intrigues, and care,
The causes of my ruin and despair ;
Oh take compassion, Time most justly dear,
Upon a heart repentant and sincere !
Oh wherefore, &c.

VIII.

Thus once again I would begin to live,
And with new hopes for better objects strive,
No moment of the day should then be pass'd
Without employment worthy of the last ;
That death might find me well prepared and fit
For the last journey, as the world I quit.
Oh joy unspeakable ! how blest were I
If thou, oh Time, would'st listen to my cry !
Then wherefore dost thou not return again,
Time past and wasted, Time bestow'd in vain ?

NOTE.

A subsequent note of Dr. Scott's, after emancipation had
been granted, was as follows :—

  " But some one may argue thus—' Be it as you say—of
what service can it now be to the country, to write about Roman Catholic securities ? Causa finita est ? Emancipation has
taken place, would you repeal concessions and recall the grant ?
Nor was emancipation conceded without attention being paid
to your question of distinction between canons of faith and
discipline. It was frequently discussed in Parliament from
1810 to 1813. Mr. Grattan, in the year 1812, moved for a
Committee to investigate those points, but the House refused to
grant one. In 1813, the same motion was again brought forward, and again rejected after a long discussion. Mr. Canning
in both years speaking decidedly against it, although it was

ably supported by Sir J. C. Hippesley, who brought it forward
in the latter year.'

" In answer, I beg leave to declare—that although I never
was an advocate for the exclusion of our Roman Catholic christian brethren from the enjoyment of political liberties together
with ourselves ; yet, speaking as an individual, had I possessed
the power of denial, I would never have consented to their enjoyment of them, without obtaining from them such securities
for the protection of the State as they might well afford to give
us, without any violation of conscience whatsoever.   It is true
that various discussions took place in the House of Commons
relative to the distinction between Canons of faith and Canons
of discipline ; and it is but too true that all consideration of
them in a Committe of Inquiry was twice, and in two different
years, refused by considerable majorities of the House of Commons, led and supported by Mr. Canning.   But neither a majo-
rity in the House of Commons, nor the eloquence of Mr. Canning,
can add one iota of strength to weak and unfounded arguments,
justly measured and weighed in the mind after the excitement
of the times and the heat of debate have passed away.

" Mr. Canning was a great man, and possessed vast abilities,
and no one could hold converse with him in public life, nor
listen to his animated voice in the public senate, without feeling the fascination of his powers.   But though so highly gifted
a person, he was in matters of theology deficient even to ignorance.   It formed no part of a statesman's study in his day, nor
of the bygone days just preceding the time of his own career.
Pitt was a greater man than Canning, and yet I believe him to
have been at fault on the same subject, or he would not have
consulted the foreign universities as to the deposing power of
subjects forming a tenet of the Roman Catholic faith.

" I have said that Mr. Canning's reasons for rejecting all inquiry
into matters of faith and discipline were unfounded, because

he treated the inquiry as useless and impracticable, as even ridi-
culous, and laid it down that the Committee would have to read
through never-ending folio volumes of divinity, with contend-
ing authorities, and the whole Bibliotheca Patrum, &c.; whereas
this battle of the books was the mere chimera of his own brain,
for two or three volumes on the Jus Ecclesiasticum of Germany,
and Bossuet's Dissertation on the Gallican Liberties, would have
sufficed to open the eyes of the Committee ; while St. Augustine
with his powers of eleven folio volumes, and St. Thomas Aqui-
nas with all his host of eighteen, &c., cum multis aliis—might
have slept in their quarters undisturbed, and not been permitted
to come forward and frighten away the Committee.

    " As the matter now stands, I hold it my duty to declare—
' Causa non finita est'—that it never can and never will be
settled, until the subject be better understood by the government of this country."

Pardon, Printer, 25, Church Street, London.